WHITE SUPREMACY GROUPS

Claire Kreger, *Book Editor*

Daniel Leone, *President*
Bonnie Szumski, *Publisher*
Scott Barbour, *Managing Editor*

**GREENHAVEN
PRESS®**

THOMSON

San Die   leveland
New Haven, Conn. • Waterville, Maine • London • Munich

THOMSON

✳ ™

GALE

LIBRARY OF CONGRESS CATALOGING-IN-PUBLICATION DATA

White supremacy groups / Claire Kreger, book editor.
    p. cm. — (At issue)
Includes bibliographical references and index.
ISBN 0-7377-1365-8 (pbk. : alk. paper) — ISBN 0-7377-1364-X (lib. : alk. paper)
    1. White supremacy movements—United States. 2. White supremacy movements—United States—History. 3. Terrorism—United States. 4. Racism—United States. 5. Hate groups—United States. 6. United States—Race relations. 7. United States — Ethnic relations. 8. United States—Social conditions—1980–
I. Kreger, Claire, 1973– . II. Series: At issue (San Diego, Calif.)
E184.A1 .W3963 2003
305.8'034073—dc21   2002067166

Printed in the United States of America

Contents

Introduction

White supremacy groups are changing as members become less traditional and decentralized. Along with the shift in *who* joins white supremacy organizations is the shift in *how* these groups operate. Secret meetings at group members' homes are becoming less popular as hate groups are finding it more convenient to communicate with like-minded individuals all over the world through e-mail and racist websites. The new millennium marks the beginning of the age of the lone wolf terrorist and the terrorist cell. As racist activity shifts from group-centered organizations to isolated acts of terrorism, white supremacy groups are increasingly mimicking the organizational style and actions of radical fundamentalist religious organizations. College educated, technologically savvy members are becoming more prominent in the movement, and female indoctrination into various white supremacy organizations is on the rise.

The lone wolf terrorist

Lone wolf terrorism was affirmed as a viable means to carry out the white supremacist agenda of racial purification by Timothy McVeigh's bombing of the Alfred P. Murrah Federal Building in Oklahoma City on April 19, 1995. One hundred sixty-eight people were killed, many of whom were children who attended a day care center in the building. McVeigh was reportedly inspired to park his van filled with explosives in front of the building after reading white supremacist leader William Pierce's, *The Turner Diaries.* In *The Turner Diaries,* Pierce outlines how to create layers of secrecy within the white supremacy movement—an essential ingredient in McVeigh's success—as well as how to make bombs. McVeigh specifically chose the federal building because there were children in it. The message from the lone wolf is clear: "I am willing to kill your children for my cause." Timothy McVeigh was convicted in 1997 of the deadly attack and subsequently executed in 2001.

Terrorist cells

Terrorist cells, groups of six or seven individuals united to carry out a specific task, are also becoming more prominent as large white supremacy groups come under closer scrutiny by the federal government. Individuals within cells receive instructions from leaders with code names whom they may never meet in person. According to Alex Curtis, who maintains the San Diego–based white supremacy website, whiteracist.com,"The advantage of lone wolf and small cell activity is that it is untraceable and is the best use of our meager resources." According to Richard Firstman's May 2001 article in *Family PC,* Curtis "openly discussed assassination and filled his website with strategies for 'lone wolves,' radical racists who act alone or in small groups so as not to jeopardize the larger movement."

Often, cell members do not meet each other until minutes before an attack, as was the case for many of the nineteen men who carried out the terrorist attacks against the World Trade Center and the Pentagon in the United States on September 11, 2001. The hijacking of American airplanes and the substantial loss of lives that occurred as a result of this terrorist attack has become the new model for American white supremacy groups. Billy Roper, of the white supremacy group National Alliance, said of the September 11 attacks, "I wish our members had half as much testicular fortitude."

The surprising success of the Taliban fundamentalist's attack against Americans has provided white supremacy groups with strange mentors and allies—radicals of Middle Eastern descent, previously considered by white supremacists as members of the "mud races." White supremacy groups and members of the Taliban are united in a common cause—hatred of, and violence against, Jews. According to Michelle Cottle, writing for the *New Republic*, "White supremacists and Islamicists like Osama bin Laden just plain agree on a lot of things—in particular, that globalism and multiculturalism are the uber-enemies, and that separatism and cultural purity are the answer."

Anonymity within the movement

Anonymity has become a significant element of success in carrying out all kinds of terrorist missions. Traditional ways of doing business, such as openly recruiting, often undermines a mission well before it has begun. Open recruitment—talking to people on the street and posting fliers with meeting information—leaves white supremacy organizations vulnerable to infiltration by law enforcement agencies. Avoiding such easily scrutinized methods can help white supremacy groups avoid being traced by watchdog groups and the FBI. Indeed, white supremacy is difficult to detect and to combat when white hoods are replaced with white business shirts. According to David Ostendorf, writing for the *Christian Century*, "Standing up to white-sheeted Klansmen is one thing . . . these [neo-Nazi leaders] may be, after all, the folk with whom we work and worship, folk who are not blatantly racist and anti-Semitic, whose stance on government or guns may seem within the realm of mainstream politics."

Technologically sophisticated communication and recruitment

Anonymity within the white supremacy movement is also made possible with the help of technologically savvy members. Websites such as those hosted by white supremacy organizations Stormfront, Aryan Nations, World Church of the Creator, White Aryan Resistance, and The National Association for the Advancement of White People offer a portal through which lone terrorists may communicate anonymously with one another. Members go online to set up financial backing for a terrorist attack—or to arrange lodging while traveling to research a potential target. These online arrangements do not necessitate face-to-face contact and thus provide a way of conducting white supremacist activity that is more difficult to monitor.

Another sophisticated tool that white supremacy groups use is white power music. White power music is gaining popularity among youth worldwide. There are entire record companies dedicated to the production and promotion of bands that play "hardcore," racist rock. The allure of the angry-sounding music often entices the loner teenager before he or she recognizes the significance of the lyrics. Sometimes the lyrics themselves are the draw. Teenagers who feel alienated by their peers are most susceptible to hate rock's message of solidarity and pride in the white race. Bands with names like "RaHoWa," which stands for "Racial Holy War" repeat the phrase "we will win" in their songs as a battle cry that appeals to both a loner teen's anger and his or her desire to belong.

The new white supremacist

Further evidence of the changing dynamics of the white supremacy movement is that more women are joining various racist organizations. The traditional role for women within white supremacy circles was as "Aryan breeder." The Aryan breeder was brought into the organization to marry a virile man and to give birth to (preferably male) children in order to populate the movement from within, as recruiters attempted to populate from without.

Whether a change in social consciousness is responsible or some other factors are at work, more women are moving out of Aryan breeder roles and into positions of power. More college-educated and professional women are being drawn into the movement as well. Although the reasons for this shift are unclear, according to the Anti-Defamation League, which works to ensure fair treatment for all U.S. citizens, "Some female extremists promote women's performance of domestic tasks to aid the movement, while others encourage women to work and become politically active. However, all are demanding to express their views and agreeing that women have a significant role to play."

It is clear that the white supremacy movement is changing, but it is difficult to gauge whether these changes will result in more potent white supremacist activity. To be sure, much of the change that has occurred has made such activity more difficult to monitor and stop. The authors in *At Issue: White Supremacy Groups* present various views on white supremacist activity, including changes taking place within the movement.

1

White Supremacy Groups Use Terrorist Attacks to Recruit New Members

Brad Knickerbocker

Brad Knickerbocker is a staff writer for the Christian Science Monitor.

In the wake of the September 11, 2001, terrorist attacks against the United States—in which terrorists bombed the World Trade Center and the Pentagon—white supremacist groups are finding it easier to recruit new members. Leaders in white power groups use the attacks as proof that the U.S. government acts on behalf of Jewish people, which is detrimental to non-Jewish Americans and American interests abroad. Experts suspect that terrorist groups in the Middle East and white supremacist groups in the United States are in contact with one another, working together against what they perceive as a common enemy: the U.S. government and Jewish people.

Hate groups around the United States are using the [September 11, 2001,] terrorist attacks [on the World Trade Center and the Pentagon] to promote their causes.

White supremacists, Christian Identity adherents, neo-Nazis, conspiracy theorists, skinhead groups, and other extremists are citing the events of Sept. 11, 2001, (and since) to recruit new members—especially young people.

Many claim that the attacks on the US are the result of "the US government acting on behalf of the Jews instead of on behalf of the American people." This is one of the more subdued charges made by William Pierce, head of the West Virginia-based National Alliance, on his website. Mr. Pierce is also author of the book [*The Turner Diaries*] about race war that supposedly inspired Oklahoma City bomber Timothy McVeigh.

Such messages are seen in leaflets handed out at public gatherings, on Internet postings, and as part of the lyrics to "white-power music."

One recent development in recruiting is shortwave radio. A shortwave receiver is far cheaper than a computer, and hate-filled messages (some ad-

From "Hate Groups Try to Capitalize on September 11: Some Extremists Say Immigrants Threaten 'Aryan Race,' Others Praise Terrorists' Strike," by Brad Knickerbocker, *Christian Science Monitor*, November 21, 2001. Copyright © 2001 by *Christian Science Monitor*. Reprinted with permission.

vocating violence) now are heard on 1,100 hours of broadcasting a month across the US, according to the Southern Poverty Law Center.

It's difficult to know for sure how effective such messages are. But experts are concerned that as the mostly-secretive world of hate shifts from robes and pointed hoods to cyberspace and cable TV, the message is at least being heard by more and more people susceptible to its message of exclusion, racial superiority, and violence.

White supremacists . . . and other extremists are citing the events of Sept. 11, 2001 . . . to recruit new members—especially young people.

In its recent report, "State of Hate: White Nationalism in the Midwest," the Center for New Community, a faith-based human rights organization in Chicago, details 338 such groups across the Midwest, many of which are actively recruiting young people.

This includes 95 neo-Nazi and racist skinhead groups, a 30 percent increase over the past two years. Pierce claims that his National Alliance has seen a 50 percent increase in website visits over the past year.

Old message, new twist

Much of the hate propaganda is merely the same old message with a new twist.

"As the bombs rain down upon Afghanistan, let us remember that it is the Jewish Occupational Government in Washington, D.C., that is gaining most by this event and that any victory in this campaign accrues to the benefit of the enemies of our White Racial Loyalist idea," writes Matt Hale, head of the World Church of the Creator in East Peoria, Ill., on the group's website. "As was the case with his father, George W. Bush is determined to spread his so-called 'New World Order' around the world making the world 'safe' for Jewish supremacy and corporate profits."

"Is Our Involvement in the Security of the Jewish State Worth This?" reads a headline next to a photo of the collapsing World Trade Center in *National Alliance* magazine.

Many such groups focus on the growing number of newcomers to the US as a threat to the "Aryan race," particularly in the weeks following the recent terrorist attacks.

"They're blaming immigration for the events of Sept. 11," says Devin Burghart, author of the Center for New Community's report. "They're out there trying to mobilize on that very issue."

Even before the recent attacks, such groups were seen as a danger to domestic security.

"On the national level, formal right-wing hate groups, such as the World Church of the Creator and the Aryan Nations, represent a continuing terrorist threat," former FBI Director Louis Freeh told the US Senate Select Committee on Intelligence in May 2001.

But in a new and somewhat ironic development, some right-wing radicals find themselves supporting terrorists they might otherwise lump together with what they consider to be subhuman "mud people."

The Aryan Nations proclaims the Middle Eastern attackers in New York, Washington, and Pennsylvania to have been "Islamic freedom fighters."

Tie between white supremacists and terrorists abroad

There may even be ties between US hatemongers and terrorists abroad. Intelligence officials know of such connections dating back to at least 1987, when a meeting of US white supremacists and Arab radicals—united in their opposition to Israel—took place in Libya. More recently, a meeting between US and European Holocaust deniers was to have taken place in Beirut. But under pressure from American Jewish groups, the Lebanese government refused permission for the meeting.

Still, the messages of Pierce of the National Alliance, former Ku Klux Klan leader David Duke, and other right-wing extremists have been broadcast from Iran and Iraq.

"We are also concerned with some people in the Middle East who have begun reproducing the propaganda of American right-wing extremists—alleging Israeli complicity in the 9/11 attacks, for example," says Mark Pitcavage of the Anti-Defamation League, a historian specializing in antigovernment radicals.

An anthrax connection?

Some observers see the possibility that US extremists may have been in cahoots with foreign sources to plan and carry out the recent anthrax attacks [in the months after the September 11, 2001, attacks].

"US government experts do not seem to have seriously considered the possibility that Middle Eastern terrorists might have slipped some weapons-lab anthrax to a right-wing ally in the US," says Chip Berlet of Political Research Associates in Somerville, Mass., a leading authority on such groups.

There is also concern that European right-wingers—philosophical soulmates of the National Alliance, Aryan Nations, and other US white supremacist organizations—may have helped Osama bin Laden. Ahmen Huber, a Swiss national reportedly connected to both Islamic fundamentalism and the neo-Nazi movement there, was questioned last week about his financial support for Mr. bin Laden's Al Qaeda terrorist organization.

2

White Supremacy Is a Leaderless Movement

Howard L. Bushart, John R. Craig, and Myra Barnes

Howard L. Bushart is an instructor in the Alcohol and Drug Abuse Counselors Program at Lee College in Baytown, Texas. John R. Craig is a freelance journalist and a literary agent in Houston, Texas. Myra Barnes is an English teacher in Baytown.

Timothy McVeigh's 1995 bombing of the federal building in Oklahoma City forced Americans to open their eyes to white supremacy's new revolutionaries: the individual terrorist and the terrorist cell—a small group of people linked together for a common cause. Backed by scriptures describing "cells" of six or seven members, along with the ease of anonymous communication the Internet offers, lone racists and small pockets of revolutionaries are becoming the new activists of the white supremacy movement. Cells are difficult for the FBI to monitor, infiltrate, and destroy, and lone terrorists are nearly impossible to detect, which causes this new wave in white supremacy to grow more powerful as it becomes less visible.

W hat was Timothy McVeigh thinking?

The surprisingly speedy trial and conviction of the key Oklahoma City bomber did not answer this question to the satisfaction of many Americans. And, for many if not most of us, it is a question that nags our consciousness like a willful child demanding attention. McVeigh, it seems, was an angry man. He was angry about Ruby Ridge [1992 standoff between white separatist Randy Weaver and federal agents]. He was angry about Waco. [In 1993 the Bureau of Alcohol, Tobacco, and Firearms raided the Branch Davidian compound in order to serve its leader, David Koresh, a warrant.] He did not like what he saw happening in the United States. He was unhappy about the direction in which his country was going. He felt oppressed and abused by the government and felt he personally had to do something.

And indeed he did do something.

In 1978 William Pierce wrote the fictional *The Turner Diaries* in which a federal building was bombed. In 1995 after reading the book, Timothy McVeigh did just that, in the process killing 168 innocent Americans, which, according to the racialists, was unfortunate but unavoidable in wartime. Like the fictional Earl Turner, one angry man defied the Evil Empire, ZOG [Zionist Occupational Government], the Synagogue of Satan [all three terms refer to the American government]. By choosing the anniversary of the Waco disaster to create a new disaster in Oklahoma City, McVeigh established a new symbol for the militant right to bear as a standard into the continuing battle.

Would-be revolutionaries

Before April 19, 1995, it was David Koresh who was for many in the movements the symbol of resistance to government oppression. Certainly, he was a symbol of righteous resistance for McVeigh. Why did this man, David (Vernon Dean Howell) Koresh, who was not Identity [those who believe the white race is the true Israel] or even overtly militant, so capture the minds of the militant right? Defending his beliefs with his life, David Koresh and the Branch Davidians not only defied the United States government, they forced the government to reveal to the world its ineptitude, its disregard for human life, its arrogance, its duplicity. David Koresh, as far as his supporters in the movements are concerned, tore the mask from the pretender government. David Koresh exposed the face of ZOG.

> *Timothy McVeigh is not the first, nor will he be the last, to turn to violence in order to create change.*

White Christian patriots consider their battle plan reciprocal, since they intend to defend the nation as strongly as the Evil Empire is plotting to destroy it. Taking up the Davidian mantle of resistance, including the knowledge that innocents must be sacrificed, men like Timothy McVeigh add their name to the list of patriot martyrs.

Many throughout history have resorted to similar violent measures to rouse their countrymen to action, a course not all historians agree is the most effective means. Timothy McVeigh is not the first, nor will he be the last, to turn to violence in order to create change.

Truman R. Clark, a professor of history at Tomball College near Houston, claims that if these men had studied history, they would have known their acts would not start a revolution. In his 8 June 1997 *Houston Chronicle* article "McVeigh, Other Would-Be Revolutionaries Ignored History," Clark cites other incidents such as the 1920 Wall Street bombing against the capitalist bankers and the 1910 Los Angeles Times bombing against the virulently anti-union publisher Harrison Gray Otis, the murders committed by Charlie Manson and the bank robberies of the Symbionese Liberation Army led by Donald "Cinque" DeFreeze, all abortive attempts to start a revolution. If the bombers had known their history, Clark says, they would have known their violent acts wouldn't accomplish anything or motivate anyone.

Many Americans will readily agree with Clark, others just as surely will not. Many will voice no public opinion. They will speak of nothing controversial, join no revolutionary organizations. They will pay their taxes and express no overt anger at government policies. Instead, they will quietly sit at home reading *The Turner Diaries* and vitriolic antigovernment essays on the *Stormfront* web site, study the Bible and listen to White Power messages on shortwave radio. Some will act on their own to fulfill the predictions made by others, more violence will be in the news, and again the search will be on. But in the ranks of the leaderless resistance, there are no organizations to identify, no chains of command, no leaders to blame.

McVeigh, it was argued by the prosecution, was steeped in conspiracy theory and the radical thinking of the far right. McVeigh, the prosecution contended, was guilty of 168 counts of premeditated murder through which he hoped to start a revolution. And in the judgment of most Americans, McVeigh was guilty of murder, although unsuccessful in this attempt to provoke armed revolt. Still, the detonation of the explosive device and the devastating consequences are now stamped upon the contemporary American mind with indelible ink. Though we Americans may, as is our national wont, put it behind us and move forward, we as a nation will not forget the heretofore most savage and destructive expression of civil and political dissatisfaction ever perpetrated by one alienated individual within our borders. And, of course, it is quite tempting to take comfort the knowledge that McVeigh was simply one alienated individual.

Comforting, but not true.

Nameless, faceless soldiers

"As far as I'm concerned," says Cadillac John [member of the White Camelia of Texas, a branch of the Ku Klux Klan], "Oklahoma City is just another example of the leaderless resistance. I don't feel bad about what happened in Oklahoma. It was bound to happen and it's going to happen again and again. Americans are getting fed up and, once they do, they don't need anybody to tell them what to do."

> *In the ranks of the leaderless resistance, there are no organizations to identify, no chains of command, no leaders to blame.*

Cadillac John, like many on the racialist right, disagrees with the government's position that McVeigh, in addition to seeking revenge for Waco and Ruby Ridge, hoped to start a revolution. In fact, many maintain that a revolution is already under way and has been for some time. Timothy McVeigh, in their eyes, is but one of many soldiers, nameless and faceless for the most part, who are fighting and will continue to fight the war against ZOG, against One-World Government, against the Evil Empire. Such nameless and faceless warriors are the soldiers of the Leaderless Resistance. And, as one member of the movements notes, "There are thousands of Timothy McVeighs out there."

Of course, as previously noted, not all revolutionaries are bombers and out for blood. Not all seek warfare in the streets or an armed overthrow of the existing system. However, this does not mean that nonviolent organizations may not employ some of the tactics of leaderless resistance or that they are not dedicated to their particular cause. Such is certainly not the case. Posse Comitatus and the Montana Freemen, although both express a willingness to use violent force when push comes to shove, have resisted the might of government by challenging the government's right to enforce certain laws and standards on individual citizens. Both organizations have, for instance, formed citizen courts as alternatives to the present judicial system. Both have issued warrants for federal, local and state officials, both recognize no higher legislative power than county government, both tie up the courts with liens and lawsuits and often work within established frameworks such as the legal system, alternative media, and other areas to give the government a fit under its own rules.

Leaderless resistance is exactly what one might imagine—that is, if one imagines small, armed, militant groups, independent of each other, autonomous, but all fighting for the same cause.

Some of these revolutionary tactics may best be described as harassment tactics through which the system is challenged in such a manner that it must confront itself. For instance, the Constitutionalists pore over legal documents, laws, legislation and countless volumes of case studies, comb government policy, tie up the courts, overturn decisions and basically make the agents of ZOG either eat their own words or effect positive changes.

The Republic of Texas

The Republic of Texas, for instance, a non-racialist separatist group claims that Texas was brought into the Union illegally, that there was no proper annexation of the sovereign territory. And, since Texas was illegally annexed, federal law does not apply in the state, which is in reality still a sovereign territory although occupied by a foreign and illegal government. A former Deputy Harris County Attorney who has investigated Republic of Texas notes, "Like it or not, they raise some valid Constitutional issues." Members of ROT issue their own identification, refuse to pay taxes, refuse to carry a DPS [Department of Public Safety] driver's license, issue their own license plates and have embarked on a campaign of filing lawsuits against state, local and federal government agencies, issuing challenges and depositions to government officials, and filing property liens which have snarled the courts in a most significant manner. State Attorney General Dan Morales has gone public with his intent to vigorously prosecute those whom he accuses of filing "frivolous" claims and suits against the state with the intention of creating problems for the court system and government.

One member of the Republic of Texas finds this amusing. "Yeah, right," he says laughing. "You know why Dan Morales won't do anything about any of this? He *can't* do anything about it. Unless of course, they want to pass fair laws, tear down this sewer of a legal system we have and replace it with a system beneficial to the welfare and well-being of the citizens. It's their system. No one is doing anything at all illegal."

Aryan Nations have overtly declared their "state of war" with the powers that be and have a stated agenda of a separate homeland.

In the long run, such organizations may have a more realistic chance of creating changes within the system than do the armed revolutionaries of the leaderless resistance. However, the odds regarding success do little to inhibit the zeal of the warrior activists of the racialist right.

Timothy McVeigh, purportedly a student of the *The Turner Diaries* and other racialist literature, apparently understood the concept of leaderless resistance well. Leaderless resistance is exactly what one might imagine—that is, if one imagines small, armed, militant groups, independent of each other, autonomous, but all fighting for the same cause. The concept of leaderless resistance as practiced by the supremacist movements can be credited, according to Louis Beam [Former Grand Dragon of the Texas White Knights], to the late Col. Ulius Louis Amoss, a former Naval intelligence officer, although there is scriptural basis for such resistance as well. In Beam's article titled "Leaderless Resistance" in the final issue of his publication *The Seditionist* (Issue 12, February 1992), he notes that Amoss was the first to write on the theories of this type of "cell" organization for groups he felt would be resisting a Communist takeover of the United States.

An alternative organizational structure

Leaderless resistance is an alternative organizational structure which lends itself to independent revolutionary action apart from any central control. Beam notes that in conventional power structures, there is pyramidal hierarchy, in effect, a pecking order or chain of command "diagrammatically represented with the mass at the bottom and the leader at the top." This structure is also seen in organizations such as the Ku Klux Klan and militia groups modeled after military organizations. Once such organizations are identified by agents of the federal government, the pyramid structure or chain of command is worse than useless. In fact, it is a positive detriment to any revolutionary function at all:

> In the pyramid type of organization, an infiltrator can destroy anything which is beneath his level of infiltration and often those above him as well. If the traitor has infiltrated at the top, then the entire organization from top down is compromised and may be traduced at will.

Both Beam and Charles Lee [Grand Dragon of the White Camelia Knights of the KKK of Texas] are familiar with this type of infiltration. "The feds decided a long time ago that one of the best ways to bring down an organization is not only to infiltrate it, but to place agents in position of leadership," Lee notes. "In more than twenty years with the Klan, I've seen more than one betrayal . . . and, even though I know it's possible and even likely, it's something you never really get used to. I expect traitors, but it's still painful. These people are turning against their own kind."

It is undoubtedly true that compromised Klansmen have provided a great deal of information to the federal agencies whose task it is to monitor them. And, of course, the Klan and other organizations have indeed experienced their share of federal infiltrators. The history of this type of infiltration, although reasonably justified in the eyes of both law enforcement agencies and the public at large, is ostensibly to gather information on revolutionary groups or others who might pose a threat to the peace and security of the nation. But there are many in the movements who believe that these agents, finding no revolutionary or illegal activities among their target organizations are certainly not above creating situations which can be used to destroy the groups they have infiltrated.

The militia movement

Carl Haggard, Commanding General of the United States Special Field Forces Militia, tells anyone who will listen that the militia movement is not about white supremacy nor is it about revolution. However, he also notes that more often than not, the government takes an adversarial position toward the militia and, in effect, acts toward them as if they were a hostile force rather than honest patriotic citizens. To this end, government infiltrators invade legitimate militia groups with the intention of destroying them and, once inside, act accordingly. Haggard constantly urges members of such groups to be aware of this destructive practice and to avoid attempts on the part of the government agents and others, including racialists, who would compromise the integrity of the militia organizations.

> *Any resistance organization which has centralized leadership and a hierarchical chain of command (such as a militia) is vulnerable to compromise through infiltration.*

But there are any number of groups in America today which are undoubtedly revolutionary, and some militia groups are included among them. Some, like Aryan Nations, have overtly declared their "state of war" with the powers that be and have a stated agenda of a separate homeland. Others, such as the now-defunct The Order and National Alliance have an agenda which includes the dismantling or overthrow of the present government. However, it is an extremely formidable task to carry on a guerrilla war against such a resourceful foe as the federal government when the front-line forces of the resistance are centrally organized in a chain of command that follows the pyramid structure.

This organizational problem was experienced by West Virginia's Mountaineer Militia. Seven members of the Mountaineers, led by Floyd

Ray Looker, were arrested in October 1996 in connection with an alleged plot to bomb the FBI's National Information Center building, a repository for fingerprint files. FBI sources confirmed that they had been monitoring the group from the inside for quite some time and acted when they did because they were aware of the group's plan to transport a large amount of explosives across state lines. The decision to make arrests was made in large part because federal agents feared losing track of the explosives and placing the public at risk.

Anonymity is the shield and first line of defense for
. . . small revolutionary cells.

The pervasiveness of federal access to resistance organizations is a reality.

As far as Beam is concerned, any resistance organization which has centralized leadership and a hierarchical chain of command (such as a militia) is vulnerable to compromise through infiltration. He contends that federal resources are such that once they identify any organization or any individual as a threat, the days of that organization or individual are numbered. However, in established resistance groups where organization is extant, the government has a vested interest in keeping all its revolutionary "eggs" in one basket. And as long as all the eggs are in one basket, or in a limited number of baskets, they are much easier to account for.

"If I had it all to do over again," Charles Lee states, "I probably would not go public. Don't get me wrong, I don't regret joining the Klan and I certainly don't regret standing up for what I believe in. But it's been pretty tough at times. Sometimes I don't remember what it's like to not have someone breathing down my neck and watching my every move."

The members of the movements do note that leaders such as Charles Lee and long-time members of groups such as the Klan or Aryan Nations have gained a notoriety in law enforcement circles that precludes a normal life and inhibits any "terroristic" activism in which they might otherwise engage.

"I do not advocate lawlessness," Lee notes. "I do not encourage people to threaten, kill, bomb or any of the other things I've been accused of. Like that Dan Morales thing. But—even if I wanted to—I couldn't. I'm too high-profile. It's absolutely suicidal for any racialist who's been identified by the government to consider, much less act upon an impulse like that."

Anonymity is the first line of defense

Lee contends, as do most of our subjects, that the downfall of many white Christian patriots has come about because those individuals do or say something to attract attention to themselves. Gordon Kahl, for instance, made the mistake of recruiting for Posse Comitatus and appearing on television urging taxpayers to stop paying taxes and resign from the government. In addition to becoming high-profile, many make the mistake of trusting too easily. The small cells of the leaderless resistance scheme of organization address both of these problems.

Anonymity is the shield and first line of defense for such small revolutionary cells. There is no high profile inasmuch as there is no public recruiting. There are no rallies, conventions, gatherings or outspoken leaders. Where such a system is extant, law enforcement often has an extremely difficult time determining a starting point for any investigation. The racialists maintain that the best and most effective tool such agencies have to use against them is the inside informant. In the small cells of the leaderless resistance, where recruitment is done very carefully and selectively by those who compose the cells, such risk of infiltration is kept to a minimum. Even where there is successful infiltration of a cell, only this small unit of resistance is compromised and not the movement as a whole.

If one follows this line of reasoning, then it makes sense that, as Beam observes, the last thing those who monitor and compromise the activities of revolutionary groups would like to see is a "thousand different small phantom cells opposing them." And, if this is the last thing the government wants, the forces of the racial right are anxious to make sure that such resistance is the first thing the government gets. Thus, the leaderless resistance, consisting of small cells of one to seven individuals with no centralized leadership, already recognizes the enemy—the government, ZOG, the players in the One-World conspiracy. And it is the contention of those on the racial right that once the enemy is identified, then no other instruction is needed.

The leaderless resistance, consisting of small cells of one to seven individuals with no centralized leadership, already recognizes the enemy—the government.

Richard Hoskins, in *Vigilantes of Christendom,* uses Bob Mathews' group as an example of both the strengths and the weaknesses of the cell and its leaders to explain leaderless resistance. Hoskins notes that Mathews recruited a small group of men into the organization he called the Bruders Schweigen (Silent Brotherhood). Bound by a sacred oath and modeled after "the Order," a fictional leaderless resistance cell from William Pierce's *The Turner Diaries,* Bob Mathews' revolutionary force met with immediate and surprising success.

The Order's war against the government included printing and passing counterfeit money to compromise the economy, forging identification documents, purchasing arms and land for arms training, robbing banks and armored cars to finance the revolution and distributing these funds to racialist organizations across the country, killing the Jewish talk show host and blasphemer Allan Berg, and other much-publicized activities which marked their brief albeit notorious career. The salient issue, however, is just how silent was the Silent Brotherhood? The small cell—nine in all—were silent indeed, and very effective, although they exceeded what is considered the maximum appropriate number of seven. Law enforcement officials in the Pacific Northwest were left scratching their heads with no idea where to even begin investigating the wraith-like group of revolutionaries which appeared, acted and disappeared again without leaving as much as a footprint.

But, as Hoskins notes, Mathews' fatal flaw came when he "confused numbers with might." As long as Mathews and company were a small cell, they were virtually invulnerable. But Mathews began to recruit. He brought more members on board than he could effectively handle and, as is often the case in such situations, one of them—Tom Martinez—was a Judas.

Law enforcement officials . . . [had] no idea where to even begin investigating the wraith-like group of revolutionaries which appeared, acted and disappeared again without leaving as much as a footprint.

And because Mathews brought the Judas on board, the organization was compromised. Mathews, thirty-one at the time of his death, paid the ultimate price for failing to follow his own game plan. But Mathews was not the only one brought down by his indiscretion. By the time the trials were over, member Bruce Pierce was sentenced to 250 years in federal prison, Randy Duey 100 years, David Lane 190 years. Did the punishment fit the crimes? Not as far as the members of the movements are concerned. The Order members who did not remain silent, who cooperated with the government and testified against their former comrades, received much lighter sentences and have all been released from prison. The prisoners still languishing in the "federal gulags," considered by the movements to be prisoners of war, are those who kept the blood oath of silence.

Had Mathews elected not to expand, had he elected to distribute funds anonymously, to keep things close to the vest, many in the movements believe he would be alive today. But, as both Hoskins and Lee note, hindsight is twenty-twenty. Hoskins does point out in his book that nothing is in vain when Aryan Christians seize opportunities to grow and learn. Thus, The Order is not just an example of the impact that a small group of dedicated individuals can have in furthering the agenda of the racialist right, but it also serves as illustration of pitfalls to be avoided by the new wave of Christian revolutionaries who will undoubtedly follow in their footsteps. And already there are such organizations active in the country today.

The Phineas Priesthood

In a two-part CBS Evening News, "Eye on America" interview, October 14 and 15, 1996, Dan Rather spoke with Walter Theode (or Thody), a member of the group calling themselves the Phineas Priesthood. Theode is presently serving a 39-year sentence for two armed robberies he committed to finance the activities of another branch of the Phineas Priesthood. The organization, in keeping with the philosophy of leaderless resistance of which it is a part, is an organization only in the loosest sense. When Rather asked how many members the Phineas Priesthood has, Theode hypothesized in regard to the size of the total organization, "I'd say there are probably no more than two hundred." And that this small membership is scattered in independent cells. "The Phineas Priesthood," Theode said, "is not and never has been, a centralized organization."

Rather responded, "And that makes it hard for law enforcement to deal with?"

"Very definitely."

Theode spoke of the deaths in the Oklahoma City bombing as "killings" rather than murder. He noted the difference as "The only thing that would make it murder is if you don't consider it a war." And, for the separatists of the racialist right, it is most definitely a war.

God's Law prescribes death for race mixers.

It is important to note that Theode's organization, the Phineas Priesthood, although it takes its name from the story of Phinehas and the race mixers Zimri and Cozbi in the Book of Numbers, does not define the concept of the modern Phineas priest. A Phineas priest is defined by actions which are based on a zeal for God, and the priest is then considered an enforcer of God's Law. Inclusion in the Priesthood of Phineas—the scriptural priesthood, not the revolutionary group—does not require a particular political belief or theological training, nor does it require membership in any particular church or organization. It does require a knowledge of the Word and the Law of God. It does require being moved by the Holy Spirit, by Yahweh. And it requires action. As God announced when Phinehas used his javelin:

> Phinehas the son of Eleazar, the son Aaron the priest, has turned back My wrath from the children of Israel, because he was zealous with My zeal among them, so that I did not consume the children of Israel in My zeal. (NUMBERS 25:11)

Thus, if men such as Timothy McVeigh and Terry Nichols, neither of whom have claimed Identity beliefs, were moved to outrage by a realization of the evil inherent in the government, and if this outrage led to violent action, righteous and justifiable by scriptural criteria, then they have participated in the *function* of Phineas priests. This is true even if they were unaware of the Spirit and how it moved them. Their works, more than any ideology, training, or ceremony, have identified them. Some in the movements would venture to state they have claimed the mantle of the priesthood in the past. But, as Richard Hoskins notes in *Vigilantes of Christendom,* those who consciously enforce God's Law in defiance of man's law are the *true* inheritors of the title Phineas priest. And the Phineas Priesthood ties in very nicely with the concept of leaderless resistance which also is described by the Scriptures.

In the Book of Ezekiel the prophet experiences a vision. Yahweh opens the eyes of Ezekiel to the abominations and iniquities perpetrated by the children of Israel who have turned from the Word, from the Law, and have allowed "strangers" (non-whites/non-Christians) to live among them and intermarry, have yielded to un-Godly government, and are engaging in widespread acts of blasphemy and self-destruction:

> Then He said to me, "have you seen this, O son of man? Is it a trivial thing to the house of Judah to commit the abominations which they commit here? For they have filled the land with violence; then they have returned to provoke Me to anger. Indeed they put the branch to their nose.
>
> Therefore I also will act in fury. My eye will not spare nor will I have pity; and though they cry in my ears with a loud voice, I will not hear them." (EZEKIEL 8:17–18)

The widespread abominations described in the passage are certainly likened to the United States of today for the faithful of the Church Militant. And, as Yahweh has revealed to the prophet the problems in the land of the Israelites, He also describes the solution:

> Then He called out in my hearing . . . "Let those who have charge over the city draw near, each with a deadly weapon in his hand." And . . . six men came . . . One man among them . . . had a writer's inkhorn at his side . . . They went in and stood beside the bronze altar. (EZEKIEL 9:1–2)

According to Hoskins, the Book of Ezekiel describes the perfect number for the enforcement of God's Law—seven. And among the six men who constitute the cell is the scribe who identifies the enemies of the Lord and marks the faithful. The seventh member, always present among the faithful, is Yahweh of Hosts ever guiding the group in its divine purpose. The purpose is clearly defined in the following passage:

> To the others He said in my hearing, "Go after him [the scribe] through the city and kill; do not let your eye spare, nor have any pity.
>
> Utterly slay old and young men, maidens and little children and women; but do not come near anyone on whom is the mark [made by the scribe to identify the faithful]; and begin at My sanctuary. So they began with the elders who were before the temple."
>
> Then He said to them, "Defile the temple and fill the courts with the slain. Go out!" And they went out and killed in the city. (EZEKIEL 9:1–7)

Thus, the methods and the motivations of the priests of Phineas are often in complete alignment with the mission of the leaderless resistance. Hoskins claims that the Phineas priests have always been among Aryan Israel and have always risen to enforce God's Law among those who would flaunt it. Their commitment to the Word is absolute: God's Law prescribes death for race mixers, Phineas priests put them to death. God's Law prescribes death for usury, Phineas priests execute usurers. God's Law prescribes death for blasphemers, Phineas priests destroy those who blaspheme. God's Law prescribes death for homosexuals, Phineas priests carry out the sentence. This is the Law as commanded by the Scriptures.

It is a widespread belief among the movements that many of the ills of the world result from failure to enforce scriptural law. Such failures are serious affronts to Yahweh and usually result in catastrophe for White Israel. Allowing in the "stranger" has resulted in oppressive and tyrannical government as freedoms and property are lost to the money-lenders. Strangers have visited White Israel with plague. The children of God have adopted the ways of the stranger and turned from Yahweh. Crime is rampant. Social upheaval is rampant. The only hope for the future is knowledge of the Law, and willingness to enforce it.

White supremacists must obey God's law

Hoskins notes that adherence to scriptural principles and the knowledge of the Laws of God are key elements which those in the movements cannot afford to overlook. To do so is to court disaster. This, he maintains is another reason The Order was doomed to failure. Bob Mathews was an Odinist, not a Christian. He did not fully understand the risks involved in working with individuals who were not dedicated Christians, who did not put the Word first.

Only in recent years have we been willing to tolerate the intermarriages with "strangers" which are common today.

In *Vigilantes of Christendom,* Hoskins includes communications from both Bruce Pierce and Richard Scutari, two imprisoned Order members to make his point. Hoskins describes how he wrote to Bruce Pierce and inquired what Pierce would do differently if he could. Pierce responded that he had come to the conclusion that "working with others is a sure sign of eventual failure." He also was unequivocal in stating that under no circumstances would he ever again cast his lot with non-Christians. Pierce is quoted in Hoskins' work as stating, "Not only would they have to be Christians, but they would have to Identify with God's Law and believe the Law-commands of God, and their life would have to manifest those beliefs."

Along the same lines, Richard Scutari responds to Hoskins' question "Would you do it again?" Scutari, too, is unequivocal in his response. "In a heartbeat! But without the stupid mistakes. I have dedicated my life to God's Laws, the meat of the Word. The motivating forces come from Laws, the meat of the Word." This, too, is the mark of a true priest of Phineas—one who knows the Word, and the Word Made Flesh and who listens to the voice of God within him—one who hears the voice and follows—with zeal. Scutari further states. "The motivating forces come from deep within my soul and I would not be much of a man if I did not act on what every fiber in my body tells me is right."

Thus, for many members of the movement, the call to Phineas priesthood is more conscription than volunteerism. It is being touched by God Himself. As Mike Hallimore notes, Phineas priests are moved by the Holy Spirit. One who executes race-mixers simply because he does not like race mixing, for instance, is not functioning as a priest of Phineas. However, one who is zealous to fulfill the commandments of God—like Phinehas of the Book of Numbers who, filled with the Holy Spirit and righteous anger, takes up the javelin and enforces the will of the Creator—this is a true Phineas priest.

Hoskins and others have observed that throughout American history, our society, based on Christian principles, has been not only intolerant of un-Christian activities, always perceived as abominations, but absolutely hostile toward them. Only in modern times have the American people rolled over to creditors who enslave not only the individual, but the nation. Only in recent years have we been willing to tolerate the intermarriages with "strangers" which are common today. Only in the past few decades have Americans stood for the slander of the Church and Christianity itself by blasphemers who wish to deny the true religion, who wish to separate the state from its divine basis. To engage in such abominations—forbidden by Yahweh—was to become lawless. To support such activities was to become a renegade. And to engage in lawlessness, to become a renegade was to die.

Hoskins maintains that this was because in former times white Christians, inwardly seething with righteous rage, would arise to enforce the Laws of God. Open homosexuals would simply disappear. Mixed-race couples would be found dead. Banks would be robbed and the wealth redistributed. Renegades, those who were "of the blood" yet violated the Law, who turned against their own people in their lawlessness, who adopted the ways of the stranger, were forced to pay very careful attention to what they did and said because they knew their days were numbered. This was the influence of the Phineas Priesthood.

Such zealots, whether they are in the phantom cells of the leaderless resistance or acting alone, are certainly a force to be reckoned with and undoubtedly a thorn in the side of the agents of ZOG. But they mostly pose a threat to anyone who violates the Laws of Yahweh, who has the temerity to insult the true God of the world, who blasphemes against Him or the faith.

Hoskins makes the observation that, even today, a renegade gives careful attention to a speaker who complains of a violation of God's Law. "The renegade is never sure," he says, "whether the one speaking is a harmless malcontent or a priest. The difference is the difference between life and death."

3

The Internet Is Changing the Face of the White Supremacist Movement

Les Back

Les Back is the head of the Centre for Urban and Community Research at Goldsmiths College in London.

The Internet offers isolated white supremacists an anonymous link to people all over the world who share white power ideology. Websites like Stormfront, the first racist site, offer chat rooms for like-minded individuals to recruit members for white supremacist groups and discuss racist ideas. The Aryan Dating Page allows white supremacists to place personal ads, while RaceLink offers a list of contacts across the world for activists to stay with when traveling. The growing racist activism on the Internet is not as dangerous as one would think, however, since commitment and follow through are lacking in many white supremacists who use the Internet as an exclusive source of contact. Nevertheless, the Internet makes it easier for white supremacists to engage in individual acts of terrorism.

After celebrating the Internet as a digital nirvana in which democracy and free speech flourish, we are finally uncovering the dark side in which racists and xenophobes not only broadcast their propaganda in cyberspace but also ply their paraphernalia and hate through international networks. However the spate of scare stories about the burgeoning tide of racist online materials ignores the ultimate question: is the face of racism changing?

Most articles focus exclusively on the number of websites, virtual discussion groups and chat rooms spreading the messages of white supremacist groups like the Ku Klux Klan, White Aryan Resistance and the British National Party, which first seized the Internet as an unregulated and relatively cheap media in the mid-1990s. While there is no doubt that these sites and groups are growing, accurate estimates are difficult to calculate.

To investigate hate on the Net, you must combine the skills of a detective, a lie detector and propaganda code breaker. For online materials are part of a digital masquerade that conceals as much as it shows. You cannot simply count and record web addresses because of the frequency in which pages are posted and taken down. However, experts agree that there are hundreds of sites, perhaps as many as 3,000.

We are finally uncovering the dark side in which racists and xenophobes not only broadcast their propaganda in cyberspace but also ply their paraphernalia and hate through international networks.

Much of the debate about hate on the Net has revolved around censorship. Internet Service Providers (ISP) may voluntarily prohibit use of their servers and install filters along with web browsers to prevent access to key racist sites. But it is almost impossible to regulate the Net as a whole. The debate about censorship has become a cul-de-sac because of the seemingly irreconcilable tension between the libertarian ethos of free speech and the difficulty in defining the limit of what is morally acceptable to say or write. To some extent, the polemic overshadows the critical issue: what is drawing people into the racist Net world?

"WHITE PRIDE WORLDWIDE"—with this slogan, Don Black of the U.S. launched the world's first and most notorious racist website, Stormfront, on March 27, 1995. Black, a former Klansman, learned his computer skills in a federal prison in Texas where he compulsively worked on the prison's Radio Shack TRS-80 computer at U.S. taxpayers' expense. Once out of jail, Black put his new skills to work to build an international system of followers by offering a trans-local notion of race.

A common language of race and white solidarity

Consider this passage from an e-mail sent to Stormfront: "I am a 20-year-old white American with roots in North America dating back 300 years and then into Europe, Normandy, France. Well anyways, I am proud to here [hear] of an organization for the advancement of whites."

Racists like Black are basically using the Internet to foster a notion of whiteness that unites old world racial nationalisms (i.e. in Europe and Scandinavia) with the white diasporas of the New World (i.e. United States, Canada, South Africa, Australia and New Zealand and parts of South America). Despite the diversity of racist groups in cyberspace, they share a common language of race and white solidarity. Firstly, this notion of whiteness promotes a racial lineage that is plotted through, and to a large extent sustained in cyberspace. The Internet is the technology of globalization, interconnecting permeable human cultures. Yet in the racist Net-world, the Internet is used to foster an ethos of racial separation. With the goal of establishing "white fortresses" in cyberspace, these racists are forging new connections between ultra right-wing sites in North America, Western Europe and Scandinavia at a considerable pace.

Yet, it is still the American websites and news groups that are the most sophisticated and the most active.

The big question remains exactly how many people are being drawn into racist activism by the Net? Recently, Alex Curtis—self-proclaimed "Lone Wolf of hate" from San Diego and producer of the extremist magazine *The Nationalist Observer*—claimed to "reach 100s–1000s of the most radical racists in the world each week." However, it is dangerous to overestimate the level of activity. The number of white racists regularly involved in the Internet globally is somewhere between 5,000 and 10,000, divided into 10 to 20 clusters. Once again, it is impossible to offer anything other than an educated guess. The number of "hits" on a web page, for example, need not indicate "sympathetic inquiries," rather they could include opponents, monitoring agencies and researchers. The key point is that these relatively small numbers of people can have a significant presence.

Not only are they using the Net for recruitment, but attempts are also being made to combine cyber-activism with that of the "real world." For example, the RaceLink web page offers a list of activists' contact details and locations around the world. Additionally, The Aryan Dating Page (now posted on Stormfront) offers a contact service for white supremacists. While most of the profiles are American, there are also personal ads from a range of countries including Brazil, Canada, Holland, Norway, Portugal, U.K., Slovakia and Australia as well as from white South Africans.

Lonely hearts in search of their own kind

One of the interesting things about scrolling through the personal ads is that the faces that appear are nothing like the archetypal image of "The Racist." There are very few skinheads with Nazi tattoos: these white supremacist "lonely hearts," mostly in their twenties and thirties, look surprisingly prosaic. Take 36-year-old Cathy, who lives in the U.S. state of Pennsylvania, which is far from an ethnic melting pot, but who is "desperate to move to a WHITE area!" She appears in the photograph in a rhinestone outfit with glitzy earrings: "The picture of me is a little overdone," she explained. "I had photos done with the girls at the office . . . I look like an Aryan Princess when I get dressed up. But I am really the girl-next-door type." Or, 19-year-old Debbie from New England, who wrote: "I am [a] young white power woman who seeks someone seriously devoted to the white power movement. A person whose commitment is undaunting. I would like to speak with men who share the same values as I."

With the goal of establishing "white fortresses" in cyberspace, . . . racists are forging new connections between ultra right-wing sites in North America, Western Europe and Scandinavia at a considerable pace.

The male ads provide an equally unexpected set of portraits of white supremacy. Frank, a 48-year-old divorced single parent from Palo Alto, California, writes: "Today I'm a responsible parent and have my views but don't go out of my way to let it be known unless confronted. I have tattoos, and am down for the Aryan race. So hope to hear from you fine ladies in the near future." Here Frank presents himself as a kind of white supremacist "new man." This is contrasted with John Botti's ad, a 25-year-old from Los Altos who presents himself as a preppy, "going places" kind-of-guy. He wrote: "I am looking for some who is as conservative and pretty as hell. Equally as important is someone with a quality education." These are images of fascism in the information age that bear little resemblance to previous incarnations. This was brought home very powerfully by the image of Max, a 36-year-old Canadian, who described himself as a "long-time Movement activist." He listed his interests as anthropology, Monty Python's humour, the Titanic story, Celtic music and [U.S.] Civil War re-enacting. Max chose to have his photograph taken at his computer keyboard, where he presents himself as the picture of technological proficiency. This struck me, the first time I saw it, as a very appropriate image of the face of today's racism.

The condensed rate of exchange in cyberspace shortens the fuse for an explosion.

However, these postmodern portraits of racism are coloured by fragmented and multiple identities little suited to the disciplined organization of "real world" racist politics. In this mercurial world, can the ideology and commitment to racism be turned off as quickly as the computer? There is some evidence to suggest that Net-racists have a rather chaotic affiliation to white power politics. For example, American Milton J. Kleim, who was once the self-styled "Net Nazi Number 1," renounced his politics almost overnight.

Shifting from national socialism to misanthropy

Kleim first became involved through Usenet, a network of online news groups, as a student in 1993. But he didn't have a face-to-face meeting with anyone in the racist movement until he graduated in 1995. Less than a year later, he abandoned racism altogether. In an e-mail interview he commented: "The act of leaving was painful, and the aftermath stressful [. . .] I essentially became a 'nonperson,' and I haven't really been denounced [. . .] I only received two or three harassing phone calls from displeased movement adherents. . . The saddest part is that my 'movement' experience was my most exciting, most rewarding time in my life," he commented. "I've moved from National Socialism to Misanthropy." Racist culture offered Kleim a sense of purpose through an online identity and a temporary resolution to existential crisis. This same sense of purpose comes through in many interviews with Net racists. What is equally true is that this does not last and the virtual mask of racial extremism can be quickly cast off.

Not only does individual commitment appear shaky, but so do the larger networks of Net-based racist groups. In the "real world," each group generally revolves around or owes its existence to a charismatic leader who takes on the initiative of forging alliances. These agreements, however, are generally short-lived because of power struggles between the various leaders. In cyberspace, this fall-out seems to be occurring at an even faster pace. Basically, the condensed rate of exchange in cyberspace shortens the fuse for an explosion. The vituperative online feud between Harold A. Covington of the National Socialist White People's Party, William L. Pierce of the National Alliance and both sets of their supporters (in the U.S.) is perhaps the best example of this syndrome. Reflecting on "The Future of the White Internet," Covington wrote:

> The Net is being viciously and tragically abused by a shockingly large number of either bogus or deranged "White Racists" [. . .] I think it is too early just yet to quantify just how the lunacy interacts with, counteracts and affects the impact of the serious political work. It is like panning for gold in a flowing sewer; both the raw and toxic sewage and the gold are there, and the question is how much gold any individual can extract before the fumes and the corruption drive him off—or until he keels over and falls in and becomes part of the sewer system.

The racist use of the Internet is not about to deliver a mass global racist movement. In this sense, the imitators of fascism and Nazism are not in the same league as the zealots of yesteryear. Yet the significance of this phenomenon should not be sought in the numbers of activists.The fact that those involved remain relatively small should not be read as a comforting statistic. What, then, is the nature of this threat? The real danger is perhaps that in the information age isolated acts of racist terrorism may become commonplace. In this respect the 1999 London bombing campaign conducted by David Copeland—who found his "recipe" for nail bombs on the Net—may be an indication of the form that racist violence will take in this millennium. These acts are perpetrated by individuals whose prime contact with racist politics is via their computer keyboards.

4

Racist Video Games Target Youth on the Internet

Anti-Defamation League

The Anti-Defamation League, based out of New York City, works to stop the defamation of Jews and to ensure fair treatment for all U.S. citizens. It publishes the periodic ADL Report, *and the* Law Enforcement Bulletin.

White supremacy groups are capitalizing on young people's love of video games by advertising and hosting racist games on their websites. Games such as "Ethnic Cleansing," "Shoot the Blacks," and "Escape from Castle Wolfenstein" are also available through white power record labels. The deplorable object of these racist video games is to kill as many Jews, Hispanics, and African Americans as possible.

Attempting to capitalize on the vast popularity of computer video games—especially among the young—hate groups are manipulating available technology to create violently racist and anti-Semitic versions of popular video games, the Anti-Defamation League (ADL) says in a new report.

With titles such as "Ethnic Cleansing," and "Shoot the Blacks," the manipulated games are proliferating on the Internet, where they can be previewed, purchased, or downloaded on the Web sites of some of the nation's most dangerous hate groups. These so-called "White Power" games are advertised as "entertainment" on extremist sites run by neo-Nazis, white supremacists and Holocaust deniers.

"Once again, racists are finding new ways to exploit technology to spread their message of white supremacy, anti-Semitism and hate to a mass audience," said Abraham H. Foxman, ADL National Director. "As with most computer games, these games are being created primarily for a teenage audience. The difference is these games are loaded with blatantly racist messages and themes. It's a disgusting, sick perversion of the original games, where the manipulated versions give players points for killing as many non-whites and Jews as possible."

From "ADL Report: Growing Proliferation of Racist Video Games Target Youth on the Internet," by The Anti-Defamation League, www.adl.org, February 19, 2002. Copyright © 2002 by The Anti-Defamation League. Reprinted with permission.

Several hate groups have invented new game levels and characters by taking advantage of a built-in feature of some commercially sold games that enables them to be modified—creating "mods," in the industry parlance—of the original games. Other hate groups have created their own original racist games using "open-source" software that enables new games to be constructed essentially from scratch.

"Ethnic Cleansing"

Resistance Records, the white supremacist label of the virulently racist group, the National Alliance, is currently selling a new game called "Ethnic Cleansing," an anti-Semitic and racist game created using the powerful open-source game engine *Genesis 3D*. The makers of this software allow the game to be altered and sold as long as certain preconditions are followed, and *Genesis 3D* takes no responsibility for any alterations to the game software.

These . . ."White Power" games are advertised as "entertainment" on extremist sites run by neo-Nazis, white supremacists and Holocaust deniers.

In "Ethnic Cleansing," the player kills Blacks and Hispanics (the game uses pejorative terms) before entering a subway, "where the Jews are hiding." At one point in the game a video clip is shown featuring National Alliance leader William Pierce talking about an "upcoming white revolution." The game is offered for $14.88 on CD-ROM on the Resistance Records Web site. Racist caricatures of African-Americans, Hispanics and Jews appear throughout the game, which also contains a variety of racist symbols, including National Alliance signs and slogans.

The "Ethnic Cleansing" sound effects, described as "Realistic Negro Sounds," turn out to be "monkey and ape sounds" that play when dark-skinned characters are killed in the game's first level. Jewish characters appearing in the second level are made to shout "Oy vey!" when slain.

Resistance Records describes "Ethnic Cleansing" as "the first in a series," followed by the forthcoming, "Turner Diaries: The Game." *The Turner Diaries,* an apocalyptic racist novel written by Pierce, describes a white underground resistance army that destroys the U.S. government and takes control of the world. Among others, the book is believed to have inspired Oklahoma City bomber Timothy McVeigh [convicted and executed in 2000 for the Oklahoma City bombing].

Holocaust games

Other anti-Semitic and racist Web sites have recently created new games, or modified older games to give them a racist underpinning. Many of the altered games are visually realistic and violently racist.

The Peoria, Illinois-based World Church of the Creator, the anti-Semitic and racist group led by Matt Hale, offers several downloadable games as part of a newly created "comedy" page. The Creator Web site features several "run the concentration camp"-themed games and others in this vein. A modified version of "Escape from Castle Wolfenstein," the original "first person" 3-D shooter game, enables the player to shoot Black men, with the words "Dead N-----" appearing by their bodies. The action takes place in hallways and rooms lined with white power symbols, anti-Semitic graffiti and pictures of Adolf Hitler and Anne Frank, among others.

The World Church of the Creator's "comedy" section, which includes racist jokes, comics and media files, boasts several downloadable racist games. These "White Power Games" had been posted to a public Internet provider's site, where the files could be easily retrieved and downloaded.

The Nebraska-based neo-Nazi and Holocaust denier, Gary Lauck, offers a game where the player is challenged to shoot "Jewish" rats racing between canisters of Zyklon-B [gas used by Nazis to kill Jews during the Holocaust] and a Star of David. The setting is the Polish concentration camp Auschwitz.

Lauck, whom ADL dubbed "the Farm Belt Fuhrer" several years ago, has three games on his Web site, including "SA Man," a version of Pac-Man where the player maneuvers a Nazi figure chased by caricatures of Jews through a three-dimensional maze of buildings. The game includes "Seig Heil" sound effects and Nazi marching music. One of the leading suppliers of Nazi paraphernalia to Germany, where such material is illegal, Lauck served prison time in Germany in the 1990s for inciting racial hatred and anti-Semitism. The games include his Web site and mailing address in the opening and closing graphics.

5

More Women Are Joining the White Supremacist Movement

Jim Nesbitt

Jim Nesbitt is a former reporter with the Newhouse News Service—he currently writes and edits for an alternative newspaper in St. Louis.

Women in the white supremacist movement are moving out of the "Aryan breeder" role—in which their sole function was to bear Aryan children in order to populate the movement—and into the ranks of leadership. More college educated and professional women are turning to the white supremacist movement as it becomes decentralized and less traditional. In addition, the Internet has been instrumental in recruiting women for white supremacy organizations. Women are vocal in Internet chat rooms, as are the growing number of opponents to female inclusion.

Just who is a soldier in America's white supremacist movement might surprise you. An increasing number of professional, college-educated women are demanding a shoulder-to-shoulder role with men.

The trend represents an important cultural shift from the traditional, men-dominated view of women as "Aryan breeders" who should play a passive role and provide food and comfort to their racial warriors.

Scholars, civil rights watchdog groups and white supremacist leaders estimate women now are a quarter of the membership of many organizations and as much as half of the new recruits. And they aren't just wives or girlfriends following their men.

The new wave of white supremacy

Lisa Turner is one of them. She's college-educated, savvy about the power of the Internet, adamant about women having a voice in the cause that has captured her commitment and articulate about her core beliefs.

Those beliefs include the convictions that Adolf Hitler was a great man, the Holocaust was an overblown fraud, Christianity is a "pernicious and poisonous" doctrine concocted by Jews to shackle the white race, and whites are at the top of nature's hierarchy and should dominate the world.

She won't give her age or profession or have her picture taken. But Turner, who lives near Sacramento, California, wants the world to know that today's white supremacist doesn't always wear a hooded robe, isn't a poorly educated redneck loser and, increasingly, may be a highly motivated woman entering the movement because of her own beliefs—not those of a husband or boyfriend.

"We feel like we're a new wave of pro-white activists, and that we shouldn't be pigeonholed," Turner says. "Pro-white has become synonymous with trailer trash and dysfunctional people, and it's time for us to let people know that we're your neighbors, we're your co-workers, we're educated, we're professionals."

Scholars, civil rights watchdog groups and white supremacist leaders estimate women now are a quarter of the membership of many organizations and as much as half of the new recruits.

Turner established the Women's Frontier section of the Web site for the World Church of the Creator, a white supremacist religious organization based in East Peoria, Illinois.

An unstable transition

Turner represents several generational trends in the white supremacy movement that experts say are creating an unstable transition period:

• The movement is growing more decentralized and fragmented, making its adherents even harder to track and its groups harder to infiltrate.

• The Internet is both a prime reason for this decentralization and a primary indicator of the rising number of women. It also is the main link between domestic white supremacists and overseas racists, resulting in an international focus known as "pan-Aryanism."

• A new generation of leaders such as Don Black, former Alabama Ku Klux Klan leader, and Matthew Hale, who heads the World Church of the Creator, are using the power of the Internet to either build up organizational muscle or bypass the traditional reliance on group structure, membership lists and a charismatic leader to get the message out.

• Although anyone can use the Internet to sample the beliefs of any white supremacist group, the movement's leaders no longer are moving into the political mainstream, mostly because politicians such as Pat Buchanan are addressing issues the movement considers important: gun control, limits on affirmative action and immigration reform.

As leaders of an older generation of white supremacists die or age, the pre-eminence of men-dominated and hierarchical organizations such as the Ku Klux Klan and the neo-Nazi Aryan Nations is eroding, experts say.

And the dominant racist religion, Christian Identity, which teaches that whites of Anglo-Saxon descent are the true Chosen People of God, is sharing the stage with other creeds that aren't based on Christianity and don't emphasize traditions that limit the role of women.

The other creeds include Odinism, which features a worship of Norse gods, and Turner's World Church of the Creator, an anti-Christian, anti-Semitic belief system that teaches that whites are on top of nature's "food chain."

A less traditional approach

All of these trends create fertile ground for racist groups that are less hidebound by tradition, doctrine and top-down command structure, such as the various manifestations of the Skinhead movement. Skinhead groups such as the Confederate Hammerskins of Dallas and the American Front of San Francisco are violent anarchists by nature and have a history of being led and organized by women, says Mark Hamm, a professor of criminology at Indiana State University and author of "American Skinheads."

Free-agent "racialism" also is on the rise, thanks to the Internet.

"The trend is toward decentralization," says Black, who lives in West Palm Beach, Florida, and runs Stormfront, the pioneer white supremacist Web site he says gets 2,500 hits a day. "Anyone can work to promote our ideas without being a member of any organization. I used to be annoyed by people who didn't join my organization, but I see the advantage now."

Brian Levin, a criminal justice professor at the University of California at San Bernardino, says, "Forget looking for a new generation of leaders. The new leadership is the ideology and the technology itself. All hate is local now."

The Internet allows people who wouldn't join a Klavern [a local unit of the KKK] or neo-Nazi cell to anonymously participate in racist discussions, vent views they wouldn't dare voice at work or in their community and sample the ideological messages of a wide range of racist groups.

The Internet is . . . a primary indicator of the rising number of women.

"The majority of people helping us don't want to join a group and have no intention of doing so," Black says. "They're in the corporate world. They're doctors and lawyers."

Although some white supremacists scoff at these closeted "Net Nazis," the Internet did provide an entry ramp into the movement for Janice, 44, a single mother of three who is a fashion accessory designer living in the Northwest. She declined to give her last name or residence.

"We are your neighbors, your co-workers, we are everywhere," she wrote in response to a reporter's written questions. "A lot of time, we keep quiet unless we feel it is 'safe' from the witch hunt. That is one of the reasons I'm glad there is the Internet: We have a way to find each other and stay in touch."

Janice works as a cyber-volunteer for Black, monitoring the Stormfront message board and chat room and maintaining her own Web site for women white supremacists. She says she is nonviolent and doesn't hate other races; instead she emphasizes "white pride" and separation of the races. She favors strict immigration controls and opposes affirmative action.

Janice has taken her first step from behind the veil of cyberspace, submitting an application to join the National Alliance, a neo-Nazi organization headed by William Pierce, author of "The Turner Diaries," a novel about an American race war that has become a bible for violence-prone white supremacists and anti-government zealots.

"I realize I am coming out of the background where it is safe, but someone has to come out and speak," she wrote.

For some white supremacists, an Internet chat room is no substitute for joining a group, going to meetings and having a certificate to hang on the wall. They want a sense of belonging to something. But for some leaders, the Internet is the ultimate recruiting tool.

Even older white supremacists such as Tom Metzger, 61 . . . advocate a measure of gender equity.

"The days of going to a parking lot and placing fliers on cars is not the only way to go in the white racial movement," says Hale, leader of the World Church of the Creator. "It's much easier to put a flier in someone's computer."

The World Church of the Creator rocketed to national attention when former member Benjamin Nathaniel Smith went on a deadly rampage in July across Illinois and Indiana.

Seeking out women

Although reliable numbers on membership in the white supremacy movement are elusive, Black says the number of women appearing in Stormfront chat rooms provides a good indication of their rising participation. He estimates that a third to a half of such participants are women. He says a third of his group's members are women.

For the Knights of the Ku Klux Klan of Harrison, Arkansas, having women in key leadership roles is nothing new. When David Duke, the former Klansman turned perennial Louisiana political candidate, was national director of this Klan in the late 1970s and early 1980s, he recruited women members, says Thomas Robb, the current national director.

One of Robb's top lieutenants is Rachel Pendergraft, 30, a mother of three who gave birth to a son earlier this month [October 1999]. Her parents both were Klan members. She joined when she was 16.

"Women have always been welcomed into the Klan, but I think that women today are getting more involved in just about everything, and that crosses over into the racialist movement," says Pendergraft, who describes herself as a white separatist. "Our thoughts and contributions are desperately needed, and some of the other groups out there are beginning to see that."

Giving women a more active role in the white supremacy movement is a matter of necessity and survival, Hale says.

"Now it's do or die for the white race, and we can't afford to fight with one hand tied behind our back," he says. "We won't win while hopping on one leg."

Even older white supremacists such as Tom Metzger, 61, leader of the Southern California–based White Aryan Resistance, advocate a measure of gender equity.

But in the chat rooms of Stormfront and other racist Web sites, there are signs of strong resistance to the rise of women and the less hierarchical and doctrinaire approach of the new organizations. Hamm, the Indiana State expert on Skinheads, says there is still a cadre of leaders in their 30s and 40s who prefer the traditional doctrines of white supremacy.

Female white supremacists are not feminists

Turner, who describes herself as a petite, blue-eyed woman of German and Swedish ancestry, with reddish-blonde hair, started on the path toward white supremacist belief in the 1980s, while living in Southern California's San Fernando Valley and getting active in the immigration reform movement.

Turner blames the nation's immigration problems on what she says is a Jewish cabal that controls America's economic and political structure. She read Hitler's "Mein Kampf" and considers herself a National Socialist—a Nazi. She also read the works of Ernst Zundel, a Canadian who insists the Holocaust is an overblown fraud. In the mid-1990s, she joined Hale's World Church of the Creator.

Although women may be shouldering their way into more activist roles in the white supremacist movement, Turner emphasizes they are not feminists.

"We're not here to challenge nature's order; we think that nature's highest calling for women is to be a wife and mother," says Turner, who is unmarried and has no children. "We're simply saying that women should have a leadership role, if they choose. They should be heard."

And if a woman has to pick up a gun, so be it, she says.

"We would defend our homes, our families, our men, if it comes to that," Turner says. "I don't advocate violence, but I consider myself a revolutionary, and we think that if things don't get better, if the grievances of white people aren't addressed, if we're not listened to, then there will be horrible acts of violence."

6

White Power Music Is an Effective Recruiting Tool

Adam Cohen

Adam Cohen is a senior writer for the nation section of Time, *where he covers law and politics. He has also written for* Chicago Magazine, Chicago Tribune *and the* Harvard Law Review. *He lives in New York.*

White power music ensnares young people with pounding "hard-core" beats while spreading racist propaganda. Music works well as a recruiting tool because those who would not necessarily be drawn to the white supremacist movement by reading printed literature might be drawn in by an enjoyment of music. Once listeners are exposed to hate lyrics, it is not difficult to convince them to take the next step and join a white supremacist organization.

On first listen, the rock band RaHoWa's song When America Goes Down sounds like any bad hard-core-rock ballad. The lyrics are cheesy high school poetry: "Will our 'twained lives split asunder?/ Will our love submerge and drown?" The vocals are often mumbled and atonal. And the instrumentals have all the professionalism of a Wayne's World guitar riff. But it's not every love song that features verses in which a man assures his beloved that "the color of our skin" will become "our uniform of war"—or every rock group whose name is short for Racial Holy War.

RaHoWa's Cult of the Holy War CD, with its rants urging whites to kill "vile, alien hordes" and destroy the Jews, is typical fare for Resistance Records, the world's leading purveyor of "hate-core" music. Some other hot titles from Resistance's catalog: Nordic Thunder's Born to Hate and Centurion's Fourteen Words. The 14 words? "We Must Secure the Existence of Our Race and a Future for White Children," as the CD jacket helpfully notes.

Resistance was a struggling hate-music label when William Pierce, perhaps America's leading neo-Nazi, bought it two years ago as a recruiting medium. Pierce, head of the white supremacist National Alliance, has been a pioneer in developing multi-media hooks to ensnare young people in his hate brigades. He has used magazines, leaflets, short-wave radio, the Internet, even hate comic books. He has also used novels: Pierce, a onetime Oregon State physics professor, is best known as the author of *The Turner Diaries*, a bloody tale that may have inspired Timothy McVeigh [convicted and executed for the 1995 Oklahoma City bombing that killed 168 people].

Music can be the most effective method for attracting young people.

Even though it now operates out of a 400-acre West Virginia compound, Resistance has global lineage. The label was founded outside Windsor, Ontario, by a Canadian neo-Nazi skinhead. In 1999, after it was purchased by Americans, Resistance bought a Swedish label, Nordland Records, doubling its musical inventory.

Resistance's sales are strong overseas, where hate movements—and hate music—are on the upswing. Among the label's top markets: France, Greece, Poland and Germany—despite German hate-speech laws. The Resistance website reflects the label's internationalist bent, promoting a concert in Bologna, Italy, with hate-rockers from across the Continent, and an "Adolf Hitler Memorial Gig" in Serbia.

Pierce, 67, believes music can be the most effective method for attracting young people. It's a mass medium, and one that can reach the unsuspecting. No one is going to read one of his books or pamphlets, or even tune in to one of his radio shows, unless he or she is in the market for hate. "But people turn music on not because they are interested in the message, but because they like the sound," he says.

Resistance Records' catalog is heavy on rock, but it has branched out into genres such as "hate country" and "hate folk" music. It has a website and an Internet radio station, Resistance Radio. Whatever the music's propaganda value, hate-group monitors believe Resistance may be bringing in more than $1.5 million in annual revenues, perhaps three times as much as when Pierce bought it. "He's making money hand over fist," says TJ Leyden, a onetime hate-rock promoter who today consults for the Simon Wiesenthal Center's Task Force Against Hate. The Wiesenthal Center believes Resistance is a major funding source for the National Alliance.

For all his success with Resistance, Pierce has some qualms. Not about the lyrics calling for killing blacks and gassing Jews—he's fine with that. But Pierce, who listens to Beethoven and Tchaikovsky, knows that by selling rock he is further exposing white youth to what he regards as "black music." Rock 'n' roll has black roots, he says, and it was Elvis Presley and "the media" who brought it into the white mainstream.

So isn't Pierce worried that Resistance is polluting the nation's Aryan culture—one of his favorite charges against his enemies? No, he sighs, the damage is already done. "We've had a couple of generations of Americans raised on rock music," he says. If you want to reach young people now, he says, you have to use black music to do it.

Yet Pierce, who writes in *The Turner Diaries* about an overthrow of the Federal Government and the institution of a new "Aryan" regime, anticipates a day when Resistance Records' music will fade away. "I don't know who will end up being the Minister of Culture after the revolution," he says. "But I would hope we would salvage the best of our European traditions." In other words, cue up the Beethoven.

Pierce consoles himself that at least he has drawn the line at rock. Suburban white kids may be snapping up rap CDs, but Pierce and Resistance Records take pride in not contributing to the trend. "To introduce white kids to rap," Pierce says, "would be an abomination."

7

The Making of a White Supremacist

T.J. Leyden, interviewed by *Intelligence Report*

T.J. Leyden is a former neo-Nazi skinhead and a consultant to the Simon Wiesenthal Center in Los Angeles, California.

Bored middle class white children are the most likely young people to join white supremacist groups. Recruiters walk the streets and attend punk rock shows looking for angry youth to entice into the movement. Dissatisfied teens who are looking for a sense of belonging and someone to blame feel welcomed by the strong brotherhood that white supremacist groups offer. The newest recruiting trend is to use the Internet to entice loner children.

Intelligence Report: What brought you into the Skinhead movement?

T.J. Leyden: I was hanging out in the punk rock scene in the late '70s and early '80s, going to shows and slam dancing. In 1980, my parents got a divorce, and I started to hang out in the street. I was venting a lot of my frustration and anger over the divorce. I went around attacking kids, punching them and beating them up. A group of older kids who were known as Skinheads saw this, and I got in with them. We didn't like people who weren't Skinheads, but it wasn't really about racism yet.

In 1981, four big-time racist bands came into the Skinhead movement: *Skrewdriver, Skullhead, Brutal Attack* and *No Remorse*. We started to listen to their music, and that broke the Skinhead movement into two factions, SHARPs [Skinheads Against Racial Prejudice] and the neo-Nazi Skinheads. Since I lived in a very upper-middle class, white neighborhood, we decided to establish one of the first neo-Nazi Skinhead gangs in Southern California.

If we caught somebody black, Hispanic or Asian, we'd attack them, beat them for sure. But 90 percent of my victims were white because it was rare for somebody black, Hispanic or Asian to be walking down my street.

Probably the worst beating was at a party. A young Skinhead girl came over and said this guy, a long-hair, tripped her. We walked over to him, myself and three younger Skinheads, and we attacked him. When we were finished, we had broken his jaw, his nose and four teeth. My friend was standing on his hand, and I kicked his thumb so hard that I broke the bone and ripped the webbing.

I was a neo-Nazi street soldier between 1981 and 1988, and in that period I was probably involved in 150 to 200 fights.

IR: Did your racism come partly from your parents?

TJL: My mom was nonracist and my dad was a stereotypical man. I mean, if somebody cut him off on the freeway, if they were black, he'd use the word "nigger." That was his generation. But the racism I really learned came from my grandfather, a staunch Irish Catholic. He would say, "You don't bring darkies home" and "Jews killed Christ."

IR: What are the circumstances that lead teenagers to join neo-Nazi gangs?

TJL: We were middle-class to rich, bored white kids. We had a lot of time on our hands so we decided to become gang members. When a kid doesn't have something else constructive to do, he's going to find something, whether it's football, baseball or hanging with neo-Nazi Skinheads. I tell people all the time, "Every kid wants a sense of belonging." And what easier group to fit in with than Skinheads? You're white, you're Nazi, you fit the criteria.

If we caught somebody black, Hispanic or Asian, we'd attack them, beat them for sure.

IR: When did you start to really learn the ideology of racism?

TJL: After I joined the Marine Corps in 1988. They teach a philosophy that if you do something, you do it all the way, not half-assed. So since I was a racist, I started reading everything I could read about Nazism, World War II, Adolf Hitler. Then I started reading about George Lincoln Rockwell [founder of the American Nazi Party]. Maybe because he was American and a commander in the military, for me he was a better role model than Hitler. William Pierce [leader of the neo-Nazi National Alliance] was influential for me, and Tom Metzger [founder of White Aryan Resistance, or WAR].

Tom's more of a public speaker, able to pump people up. Pierce is better as a writer. Pierce would probably put you to sleep at a rally, whereas Tom bores the hell out of you when he writes.

IR: How did you get to know Metzger?

TJL: When I was in the Marines, I was writing to one of my friends in California, and he wrote back saying he was doing security for Tom Metzger. I said, "Wow!" Then, all of a sudden, Tom writes to me and sends me the WAR paper. So I start corresponding with him. I didn't actually get to meet him until I got out of the military [in 1990].

I was recruiting, organizing Marines to join the racist movement. I manipulated guys through little things, talking to them about Nazism on a small scale. Like the Marines never had tailored uniforms until after World War II, and then all of a sudden we were tailoring ourselves because we wanted to look sharp like the Nazis. We wanted to walk and have thunderous footsteps like the Nazis. I would take things in the Marine Corps and say the Nazis did this first.

Eventually, I was kicked out for alcohol-related incidents—not for being a racist. If you look at my military packet you're not going to find anything about me being a racist. And I had two-inch high Nazi SS bolts tattooed on my neck! Once I got cut, I decided to be a [Skinhead] recruiter. I was going to get younger kids to be street soldiers.

The recruitment process

IR: How did recruitment work?

TJL: We incited violence on high school campuses. We'd put out literature that got black kids to think the white kids were racist. Then the black kids would attack the white kids and the white kids would say, "I'm not going to get beat up by these black guys anymore." They'd start fighting back, and We'd go and fight with them. They'd say, "God, these guys are really cool. They came out, and they didn't have to."

That put my foot in the door. Then I could start talking to them, giving them comic books with racist overtones or CDs of racist music. And I would just keep talking to them, giving them literature, indoctrinating them over a period of time.

Later on, in 1993 and 1994, I started doing a lot less recruiting and a lot more military training, more gathering guns, doing surveillance on law enforcement officers, finding out which shifts the police department worked, if there were more SWAT team members in the morning or night. The aim was that if anything happened, I wanted to know when they were the most powerful and the most weak. I starting watching LAPD, DEA, ATF, SWAT videos.

We didn't have enough soldiers to overthrow the U.S. government. The only way we could attack was the terrorist way—IRA [Irish Republican Army]-, PLO [Palestine Liberation Organization]-style. Our big thing was blowing up ABC, NBC, CBS, CNN. Blow up one of those, and you get worldwide coverage.

During the L.A. riots there were 40 Skinheads who were ready to go down to Florence and Normandie and start wasting black people. What stopped them, believe it or not, was Tom Metzger. He said we didn't have enough soldiers to do something of that nature. I think Tom Metzger lost face with a lot of Skinheads because of that. They said later, "Who cares if we didn't have enough? We should have done it and hoped that it was a spark."

When a kid doesn't have something else constructive to do, he's going to find something, whether it's football, baseball or hanging out with neo-Nazi Skinheads.

IR: A spark to start a race war?

TJL: Yeah, and a whites-only North America above the Mexican border.

IR: Who were you focusing on recruiting?

TJL: I was trying to take people from a wide background, not just people in the racist movement—people who were angry about taxes, about the government. They would say, "I don't have a problem with blacks, my problems are with the government." You could find them anywhere, at a bar, a guy sitting there drinking who was pissed off at the government for what it had done to him. We had a place out in the desert where everybody went to shoot where you could find people. I would talk to these guys at bars, gun clubs, pretty much anywhere.

IR: How important are racist rock music and the Internet for recruitment?

TJL: If I filled a room with 1,000 neo-Nazi Skinheads and asked them, "What's the single most important thing that influenced you to join the neo-Nazi Skinhead movement?" probably 900 of them would say the music.

The Internet is also extremely important. Before, the kid you were going to get, eight out of 10 times, was going to be a street soldier, a kid ditching school, basically a thug. But now with the Net, you're getting the bright kid, the 11- or 12-year-old who knows how to surf [on the World Wide Web]. I'd say there are probably as many racist recruiters on the Net as there are on the street now.

What they're trying to do now is get more affluent kids. They've been trying on college campuses, and a lot of times it hasn't worked. So now they're saying, "Let's get the bright kid when he's 12, and by the time he's 18 or 19 and going into college, we've already indoctrinated him."

Leaving the movement

IR: What finally brought you to leave the racist movement?

TJL: It was an incident with my son that woke me up more than anything. We were watching a Caribbean-style show. My 3-year-old walked over to the TV, turned it off and said, "Daddy, we don't watch shows with niggers." My first impression was, "Wow, this kid's pretty cool." Then I started seeing something different. I started seeing my son acting like someone 10 times tougher than I was, 10 times more loyal, and I thought he'd end up actually doing something and going to prison. Or he was going to get hurt or killed.

I started looking at the hypocrisy. A white guy, even if he does crystal meth and sells crack to kids, if he's a Nazi he's okay. And yet this black gentleman here, who's got a Ph.D. and is helping out white kids, he's still a "scummy nigger."

In 1996, when I was at the Aryan Nations Congress [in Hayden Lake, Idaho], I started listening to everybody and I felt like, "God, this is pathetic." I asked the guy sitting next to me, "If we wake up tomorrow and the race war is over and we've won, what are we going to do next?" And he said, "Oh, come on, T.J., you know we're going to start with hair color next, dude."

I laughed at it, but when I drove home, 800 miles, that question and answer kept popping into my head. I thought that kid was so right. Next it'll be you have black hair so you can't be white, or you have brown eyes so somebody in your past must have been black, or you wear glasses so you have a genetic defect.

A little over two years after my son said the thing about the "niggers" on TV, I left the racist movement.

The Skinhead movement

IR: How would you characterize the Skinhead movement now?

TJL: Tom Metzger always says that for every kid that leaves, 100 more join. He knows that's a crock, the movement isn't growing that fast.

But these guys are becoming more adamant about terrorism. It's not a joke anymore, not when they're starting to do surveillance on families, police officers, politicians. They want to know where these guy's wives work, where their kids go to school. They're learning from the IRA and the PLO.

In the 1980s, everybody in the right wing thought The Order [a terrorist organization responsible for the murder of a Denver talk show host and the robbery of almost $4 million] was nuts. Now, you won't find one racist group out there that will oppose the [Order's 1984] declaration of war against the U.S. government.

Tom Metzger, on his hotline, says everybody should be sending Timothy McVeigh [Timothy McVeigh was executed in 2001 for the 1995 Oklahoma City bombing] Christmas cards, birthday cards, money, saying how great he is. I believe the Murrah Building [in Oklahoma City] was picked because it was a very easy federal target and it had a day care center. They wanted to send a message: "Hey, look, we're going to start killing children in this war. So I hope you're ready to die for what you believe in, because we're ready to kill your children for what we believe in."

With the [white power] music scene on the rise, you're going to get a rise in Skinheads, both anti-racist and racist. Probably 65 percent of the movement is non-racist, but even if they're not racist, they're usually into a subculture of violence. I think that you're going to see a big increase in hate crimes again.

IR: What is the relationship between neo-Nazi Skinheads and the antigovernment Patriot movement?

TJL: The militia and Patriot movements are the biggest recruitment ground for neo-Nazis. What the Patriots do is say, "The New World Order is coming." So now a kid is told by his father, "The NWO is coming, son, they're going to take away guns and free speech." The kid says, "Dad, where is the NWO coming from?" And the dad has no clue. But the neo-Nazi Skinhead walks over and says, "The NWO is The Protocols of the Elders of Zion [an infamous anti-Semitic tract that purports to show a global Jewish conspiracy]. Just take out the word 'NWO' and put in 'Jew'."

IR: What has been the personal cost of your involvement in the movement?

TJL: A little bit of my dignity. I look at myself as two people, who I am now and who I was then. I see the destruction I did to people by bringing them into the movement, the families I hurt. I ruined a lot of lives. That's the biggest thing I have to pay back. I don't forgive myself. Only my victims can forgive me.

8

Lone Wolf Terrorists Are More Dangerous than Organized White Supremacist Groups

Katherine Seligman

Katherine Seligman is a staff writer for the San Francisco Chronicle.

Lone wolf terrorists are becoming more dangerous than white supremacist groups. Lone wolves are difficult to monitor because of their low visibility and lack of social networking. Those acting as lone terrorists have carried out successful attacks, such as when Richard Baumhammers targeted Jews in a shooting spree that ended in five deaths in Los Angeles in 2000. An important tool of the lone wolf, the Internet allows such individuals who harbor white supremacist ideas to act out in the privacy of their own homes by sending hate mail to minority organizations. White supremacists who act alone cannot be linked to any particular group and are therefore difficult to detect and nearly impossible to stop.

They call him a "lone wolf," a freelance activist who takes sole credit for the nation's worst act of domestic terrorism. At a time when extremist groups find themselves increasingly infiltrated, investigated and discredited, some are reaching out to the unaffiliated to carry out their mission of revolution and destruction.

"The lone wolf, the small cell is really the wild card today," said Brian Levin, director of the Center for the Study of Hate and Extremism, based at California State University at San Bernardino. "It's problematic. They are capable of much more lethal attacks than they ever were before."

In the past, Levin said, you were much more likely to know who the terrorists were. They belonged to groups whose names were known. Now, as many hate groups tailor their outreach to lone activists, the next terrorist could be harder to detect.

In the age of the Internet, they have the perfect vehicle, watchdog groups say. While the militia and patriot movement has dwindled, hate groups grew about 10 percent last year [2000] from the previous one, according to an annual report by the Southern Poverty Law Center. And along with Web technology, their Web sites have grown exponentially. The locations on a Web site called The Hate Directory, managed in his free time by an assistant training director for the Maryland police, now print out to 50 pages.

As many hate groups tailor their outreach to lone activists, the next terrorist could be harder to detect.

They offer the freelance terrorist a buffet of extremist philosophies. Web surfers can find racist diatribes, right-wing publications and bumper stickers from a variety of sites. A number of sites glorify the lone wolf—and Timothy McVeigh [convicted and executed in 2001 for the 1995 bombing in Oklahoma City that killed 168 people], who, ensconced in the rhetoric of hate groups, reportedly wasn't an official member of any and continued to minimize the role played by co-conspirator Terry Nichols.

Racist Web sites encourage lone-wolf behavior

The White Aryan Resistance site, run by Tom Metzger, founder of the racist group and its newspaper W.A.R., features a snarling wolf with bloody teeth. Metzger calls McVeigh "our soldier." He urges followers to "believe in our race. . . . All else is up to the individual activist."

A wolf howls on the Web site run by Alex Curtis, a 25-year-old San Diego man currently in prison for a three-year campaign of harassment of civil rights and political leaders. Curtis calls McVeigh the "Lone Wolf of the Century." His publication, *The Nationalist Observer*, remains online despite his incarceration.

"The advantage of lone wolf and small cell activity is that it is untraceable and is the best use of our meager resources—no membership dues, rental of meeting halls, driving, lodging and time off for endless conventions," he writes on his lone-wolf site.

Curtis places McVeigh in the same category as Richard Baumhammers, the Pennsylvania man who targeted minorities and Jews in a shooting spree last year [2000] that killed five people, and Buford Furrow, who shot up a Jewish preschool in Los Angeles. All, he said, have "brought racial activism out of the right-wing morass."

He also provides lengthy advice for wannabe lone wolves, warning them to act alone, silently, without drawing attention to themselves. He admonishes against having bumper stickers or tattoos (makes you too easy to identify) or getting moving violations ("the urban guerrilla's worst danger").

The lone-wolf rhetoric adopted by Curtis has its roots in the "leaderless resistance" movement that emerged after two federal raids in the 1990s—the 1992 standoff at Ruby Ridge, Idaho, and the death of Robert Matthews, who founded the supremacist group The Order.

In response to the raids, Louis Beam, a leader in the neo-Nazi Aryan Nation, began to speak about a movement of "lone individuals" whose acts would snowball into a revolution. It was later embraced by Metzger and others.

The lone-wolf tactic was also epitomized in William Pierce's racist novel *Hunter,* whose hero murders interracial couples and other minorities. It's a sequel to his 1978 *The Turner Diaries,* an excerpt of which was found in McVeigh's car. Testimony revealed that he sold both books at gun shows.

"*Hunter* is to the lone wolf what *The Turner Diaries* is to armed white revolutionaries," said Levin.

Watchdog groups see the lone-wolf appeal as troubling, largely because its influence is difficult to gauge.

"Alex Curtis personifies a new kind of hater, a person who casts himself as an ideologue and agitates for violent underground campaigns against the government," said Abraham Foxman, national director of the Anti-Defamation League, when the group released a report on Curtis last fall. "The danger in his message is that it seems to be having an effect, at least among other racists and bigots who are communicating with him."

Mark Potok of the Southern Poverty Law Center said law enforcement generally did a good job of monitoring groups that planned conspiracies. But monitoring potentially dangerous individuals is a far more difficult task, law enforcement officials acknowledge.

"It is very much the era of the lone wolf," said Potok. "McVeigh ushered in that era. . . . It's very worrying. When you get a Buford Furrow who wanders into a community center and starts shooting kids, what can you do? He was a lone nut."

But Potok and others say the role of the Internet in breeding terrorists is overplayed. In general, he said, the hate sites act as "brochures." Some haven't been updated in months or years, a review of them shows. Others offer scant information except for a home page design.

Levin agrees the threat from cyberhate may be overblown, saying that in general society now is safer from extremist threats than in the '80s and early '90s when the "ideology momentum for extremism" was higher.

But today's terrorism doesn't need a broad base, he said. The greatest threat may come from an unidentified individual, someone on the fringe, an angry misfit sitting at home who may see McVeigh as a hero.

"If they can find people who are social misfits, I think the hate mongers would be very happy," said Levin.

9

White Supremacy Groups Are Expanding Their International Ties

David E. Kaplan, Lucian Kim, and Douglas Pasternak

David E. Kaplan, Lucian Kim, and Douglas Pasternak are frequent contributors to U.S. News & World Report.

American white supremacy groups and neo-Nazis abroad are developing international connections through the use of the Internet and e-mail. International ties allow racists to utilize resources that are available in other countries. For example, German hate groups now transfer their websites to the United States since they are considered illegal in Germany. Racists also find it easier to travel abroad and to find hosts in foreign countries. Some hosts provide refuge to white supremacists such as Hendrik Mobus, a convicted murderer from Germany who sought and received refuge in the United States for nine months before he was arrested in August 2000 by U.S. marshals.

When Hendrik Mobus stepped off a British jet and onto American soil last December [1999], the German neo-Nazi was looking for more than kindred spirits. A convicted murderer, Mobus needed refuge. After serving five years in a German jail for helping strangle a fellow teenager, he had allegedly violated parole by disparaging his victim, raising his arm in a Nazi salute, and organizing gatherings of the far right.

Mobus trekked across the United States for seven months, staying with suspected white supremacists in Washington State, Ohio, and Virginia. He finally landed on a remote mountaintop in rural West Virginia, at the 300-acre compound of the National Alliance, a white supremacist group that the Anti-Defamation League [a U.S. civil rights organization] calls the largest and most dangerous in the nation. There Mobus stayed for 10 more weeks, until U.S. marshals caught up with him in August 2000. He faces deportation to Germany.

A revitalization of the Nazi movement

That the 24-year-old Mobus had contacts across America is a troubling sign of closer ties between U.S. neo-Nazis and their counterparts abroad. Until the 1980s, America's postwar white supremacists were a ragtag collection of local Ku Klux Klansmen and neo-Nazis—with little exposure to people or events overseas. But in this age of globalization, white supremacists have gone international, too. Fueled by the Internet and cheap jet travel, neo-Nazi leaders are exchanging speakers and literature and forming chapters of their groups abroad. Some analysts see the outlines of a sophisticated, worldwide neo-Nazi movement, in which violent, racist groups share tactics and resources as never before. Says Mark Potok of the Southern Poverty Law Center, which monitors hate groups: "We're seeing better funding, more hiding places, and, ultimately, greater violence."

There is no shortage of people on the political fringe. German officials say some 54,000 individuals are tied to the extreme right in that country; tens of thousands more are active elsewhere in Europe. Between 100,000 and 200,000 Americans are thought to have similar ties.

Ironically, after winning the war against Nazism, it is the Americans who are helping revitalize it. For years, U.S. groups have been the major source of Nazi-inspired books, memorabilia, and propaganda; such materials are illegal in Germany but protected by the First Amendment here. Nebraska-based Gary Lauck, dubbed the "Farm Belt Fuhrer," spent two decades shipping racist literature to Germany. His luck ran out when he visited Europe, and German officials slapped him with a four-year jail term. Lauck now stays closer to home—running a Web site with a catalog, in 14 languages, of Nazi books, newspapers, and CDs.

A haven for extremists. German neo-Nazi groups are also flocking to U.S.-based Internet providers. The German government's crackdown on the far right, following a spate of violent attacks on foreigners, has prompted extremist groups there to transfer scores of Web sites to the United States. German intelligence officials say 70 percent of the nearly 400 German neo-Nazi sites are now on American servers, and nearly a third of those would be illegal under German law. In 1999, one U.S.-based Web page posted a $7,500 reward (in German) for the murder of a young left-wing activist, giving his home address, job, and phone number.

In this age of globalization, white supremacists have gone international.

Web sites and e-mail are the electronic glue that pastes together the once disparate edges of a worldwide movement. Among the most active neo-Nazi groups is Hammerskin Nation, a federation of so-called skinheads whose members sport swastikas along with their shaved heads and steel-toed boots. Known for their violence, followers of Hammerskin Nation run chapters in Australia, New Zealand, and across Europe and North America. U.S. Hammerskin bands regularly perform in Germany, while British and German Hammerskins often visit America, officials say. The Ku Klux Klan has also ventured abroad, setting up chapters in Britain and Australia and giving talks in Germany. And the Illinois-based World

Church of the Creator, whose follower Benjamin Smith went on a two-state shooting spree last year, claims chapters in Australia, Belgium, Canada, France, and Sweden.

If the American radical right has an unofficial ambassador, though, it is William Pierce, 67, leader of the National Alliance. It was at Pierce's rustic compound that Mobus was hiding. A former physics professor, Pierce wrote the notorious *Turner Diaries,* a crude novel depicting an American race war in which the U.S. government is overthrown and Jews and minorities are systematically slain. Among the novel's fans was Timothy McVeigh [convicted and executed in 2000 for the 1995 Oklahoma City bombing]; his bombing of the Oklahoma City federal building closely resembles a scene from the book.

Under Pierce's leadership, the National Alliance has established chapters in 11 countries. Pierce's travels have brought him to the United Kingdom, and since 1996 he has made four visits to Germany, where officials say he now has a representative. His main contacts are with the 6,000-member National Democratic Party (known by its German initials, NPD), a group so dominated by neo-Nazis that government officials have proposed banning it. In a speech before the party's congress in 1999, Pierce spoke of a new era of collaboration among "nationalist" groups, echoing the NPD's own calls for expansion abroad. NPD officials, in turn, have attended meetings of Pierce's National Alliance in the United States. "Our destinies are linked," Pierce later proclaimed, sounding like Adolf Hitler in 1933. "If the Jews succeed in destroying the German nation, they will have an easier time destroying us."

Like others on the far right, the National Alliance has wholeheartedly embraced the Web, offering online materials in five European languages. *The Turner Diaries,* which once had to be smuggled into Germany, can now be read on its Web site in German as well as French. Last year, Pierce also moved into the music business with the purchase of Resistance Records, reputed to be the world's largest purveyor of neo-Nazi CDs, with titles like "Too White for You" by the Angry Aryans. Pierce's warehouses reportedly carry 250 titles and stockpile some 80,000 CDs. A major market is the European skinhead scene.

American white supremacists have been "Nazified"

Despite its growing reach, however, the neo-Nazi movement remains widely fractured, both at home and abroad: Groups often hate each other nearly as much as they do non-Aryans. The danger, of course, is that even individuals, like McVeigh, can cause enormous damage. Moreover, the Internet is hastening the spread of a more consistent ideology. American white supremacists have been "Nazified" in recent years, analysts say. A generation ago, Ku Klux Klan members with memories of World War II would never have associated with Nazis; today, they attend rallies, sport swastikas, and offer sieg heils [the Nazi salute].

Such a common culture does not bode well. "All the ingredients are there," warns German political scientist Thomas Grumke, who studies the far right. "Somebody just has to mix them together."

10

White Nationalists Must Organize in Order to Protect European Americans

European-American Unity and Rights Organization

EURO is the European-American Unity and Rights Organization. It defends white interests and rights through its website, run by EURO president and former congressman from Louisiana, David Duke.

European Americans need to unite and organize their sense of nationalism and pride into established groups in order to protect white rights. Many endorse affirmative action because it helps minority groups succeed, but it is considered "racist" for whites to band together for the cause of furthering and protecting the interests of white Americans. This double standard is unfair and causes European Americans to face racial discrimination in education and employment. This discrimination will not cease unless white Americans unite under the umbrella of white nationalism. It is imperative that white Americans fight together to preserve their cultural heritage.

The European-American Unity and Rights Organization (EURO) is the national organization for the rights and heritage of European-Americans.

We maintain that the civil rights of European-Americans are being violated by affirmative action, forced integration, and anti-European immigration policies. Blacks, Mexicans, Jews and other ethnic minorities have many organizations that work for their perceived interests. Blacks have the NAACP [National Association for the Advancement of Colored People], PUSH [an organization started by Jesse Jackson that works toward social change], Urban League and hundreds of groups. Mexicans have groups such as La Raza Unita (meaning the united race). Jews have groups such as the American Jewish Congress and the Anti-Defamation League of B'nai B'rith (ADL), which supports Israel and what they see as Jewish interests both nationally and internationally. As a result of the work of these special interest groups, European-American interests are often violated by both government and media. For example, European-Americans face extensive racial discrimination in jobs and education.

European-Americans are discriminated against

We face a cultural discrimination in the media and education that consistently portrays European-Americans negatively in our relation with other racial groups. An example is the media hate crime hysteria that highlights and publicizes any White crime against minorities, but ignores the 1,000 percent greater number of Black crimes against Whites. The U.S. Government also acts against the long-term interests of European-Americans by discriminating against Europeans in immigration policies and favoring a welfare system that systematically increases the non-White percentage of the American population. Population projections by the U.S. Government now say Whites will become a minority in America by the middle of this Century. Obviously, this demographic shift will have powerful implications for the well being of European-Americans when we become outnumbered and outvoted in the nation that our forefathers founded.

We are fighting for the preservation of our heritage, freedom and way of life in the United States and much of the Western World. Ultimately, we are working to secure the most important civil right of all, the right to preserve our kind of life. Massive immigration and low European-American birthrates coupled with integration and racial intermarriage threatens the continued existence of our very genotype. We assert that we, as do all expressions of life on this planet, have the right to live and to have our children and our children's children reflect both genetically and culturally our heritage.

European-Americans now face the most extensive racial discrimination in American History. It is true that some Blacks faced discrimination in the past, but the discrimination was limited, primarily practiced in the private sector; and even then there were many businesses and educational institutions that treated them fairly. Today, the Federal Government is forcing an across-the-board racial discrimination against European-Americans in employment, promotions, scholarships and in college and union admittance. This racial bias is pervading all sectors of our national life, including civil service, education and business.

> *We maintain that the civil rights of European-Americans are being violated by affirmative action, forced integration, and anti-European immigration policies.*

The U.S. Department of Labor boasts that over 175,000 major corporations have programs favoring Blacks over Whites in employment and promotions. "Affirmative Action" is a euphemism for nothing more than blatant racial discrimination. No one should harbor the illusion that these programs simply favor equally qualified Blacks, for they consistently favor less qualified Blacks over better qualified Whites.

Examples of this practice are the *Bakke* and *Weber* Supreme Court decisions that sanctioned racial quotas. Bakke, who scored in the 90's on his tests for medical school, was denied entrance in deference to Blacks who scored in the 30's. University of Texas Law School (UTLS) Professor Leno Graglia recently showed that there were only 16 Blacks in the entire nation who deserved to attend the UTLS by scoring at least the minimum qualification scores (LSAT) of the current White students. This kind of discrimination is grossly unfair and also drives down productivity and diminishes the quality of life. Racial discrimination goes on against Whites in hiring and promotions, in scholarships and college admissions, in labor unions and contracting, both public and private.

Whites must unite and organize

Black pressure groups have not limited their attention to so-called affirmative action. They have brought about busing and forced integration of schools and neighborhoods, a program that is heightening racial tensions and drastically harming educational quality. Whites in many cities have had to remove their children from the public schools their own taxes pay for and then pay for private education so their children could be safe and well educated.

We are fighting for the preservation of our heritage, freedom and way of life in the United States and much of the Western World.

Government has forced higher taxes on productive Americans in order to finance exorbitant and wasteful welfare programs. They have practically handcuffed police and the courts, preventing them from dealing firmly with violent criminals (most of whom are Black). They have opened the floodgates of unrestricted Third World immigration, which increases unemployment and adds to already high welfare costs and crime. All these policies go directly against the interests of America's European-American population.

Groups like the NAACP have litigated and lobbied untiringly on issues they perceive as important to Blacks. On the other hand, there has been no prominent organization that forthrightly worked to defend the civil rights of Whites. Our people must come to the realization that unless we, also, organize to defend our heritage, and even our very right to exist as a people, we will lose everything of real importance to us. Under the leadership of nationally-known White civil rights leader, David Duke, the European-American Unity and Rights Organization (EURO)will receive the attention it needs in the struggle for the rights of European-Americans.

Unless European-Americans organize and act soon, America will become a "Third World" country—that is, European-Americans will become outnumbered and totally vulnerable to the political control of Blacks and other non-Whites. The same kind of population change is also going on in Canada and Europe. There are 24 all-Black countries, but there are no all-White nations except Iceland, and Iceland is not enough! There is no threat to the continued existence of the Black Race, but there is a real threat to the White. If breeds of life like the blue whale, the rocky mountain cougar, or even the tiny breed of fish called the snail darter are worth preserving, shouldn't a beautiful and creative people such as the White Race, also, be worthy of our concern?

There is no doubt that our people continued to be denigrated by the mass media, that hard-working, productive Americans are being financially stripped by high taxes for wasteful welfare programs, and that our nation is being swamped by immigration. Each of these conditions should make it abundantly clear why we need the European-American Unity and Rights Organization (EURO) to change them!

11

The White Race Must Be Preserved

Bishop Alma White

Bishop Alma White was an avid Klan supporter.

White people must do what they can to prevent racial mixing. According to the Bible, whites are the supreme race and blacks must obey them. The KKK works to protect and preserve both whites and blacks by preventing them from interracial mingling. The KKK is nonviolent and misunderstood.

White supremacy is an issue of great importance. If some of the colored people are not curbed in their ambition to mix their blood with that of the white race, it will not be long until there will be no such thing as definite racial lines. The Negroes are going north and settling indiscriminately among the whites. Property values are being depreciated by this influx of colored immigration. But little sympathy was shown the South when a race of colored slaves was liberated among them. The North had no conception of what it meant for the white people of the South to preserve the color and racial lines, considering the fact that in some places the population was about equally divided, and there was no cooperation from the North to be had in the struggle. But now, while the problem is still serious in the South, intolerable conditions are developing in some northern localities as the result of this migration of colored people.

After the Civil War, people who came south would persist in their arguments in favor of social equality. They did this chiefly because they had no solution for the racial problems, and nothing could have stirred more effectually the blood of a true Southerner who had the social problem to contend with every day in the year. Invariably, when an advocate of equality was asked if he would be willing for his daughter to marry a black man, his reply would be, "No." Where then was the consistency in his attitude toward the relationship of the races?

Theory is all right in its place, but its practicability is the proof of its merit. There are many dreamers who have advice to give; but let us hear from the people with experience. Perhaps residents in Northern states will

From *Heroes of the Fiery Cross*, by Bishop Alma White (Zarephath, NJ: Good Citizen, 1928).

be better qualified to formulate theories on a true basis after they have lived in the same locality with Negroes.

The Bible supports white supremacy

The Book of Genesis, in its account of Shem, Ham, and Japheth, sons of Noah, teaches the supremacy of the white race. Ham saw the nakedness of his father, but made no effort to cover him, and a curse was pronounced upon him and his posterity. Noah awoke from his wine and said, "Cursed be Canaan [Ham]; a servant of servants shall he be unto his brethren." "Blessed be the Lord God of Shem; and Canaan shall be his servant." "God shall enlarge Japheth [the white race], and he shall dwell in the tents of Shem; and Canaan shall be his servant" (Gen. 9:25–27). This edict was imposed by a wise and just God, and should not work a hardship on the black race. It cannot be otherwise than that it should be for their good. Until the curse is lifted from the human race, the very best position that the sons of Ham could be placed in is that of servants (not slaves), thus establishing white supremacy as foretold more than four thousand years ago.

It will not be long until there will be no such thing as definite racial lines.

At the building of the Tower of Babel God confused the languages to fulfil His purpose in working out the destiny of the races. To break down racial barriers and advocate a mixture of blood would be to subject the world to divine wrath. The only hope of civilization is to preserve unmixed the blood of the races. "If any man shall add unto these things, God shall add unto him the plagues that are written in this book: and if any man shall take away from the words of the book of this prophecy, God shall take away his part out of the book of life, and out of the holy city, and from the things which are written in this book" (Rev. 22:19).

Presumption leads to ruin and to perdition. Nothing has ever been gained by trying to change the laws of God or the penalties which He has meted out to races and peoples. There must be cooperation with His plans in the administration of justice to all mankind or the penalty will be suffered. When color lines have served their purposes, the Almighty himself will remove the barriers. This will take place some time in the reconstruction period that is coming to the whole world. Then why attempt to force the issue?

Racial mixing is wrong

It is to be deplored that there are white men of superior intelligence who would take advantage of an inferior race and sell out honor and principle to satisfy their base desires. Such men break the laws of God and man and bring ruin to themselves and their posterity. How great will be their responsibility! Their offspring must bear the stigma of criminal and degraded parentage, whether reared among the blacks or whites. This was a part of the evils of slavery, and present day conditions are as bad, if not worse.

A class of cultured Negroes have organized societies to promote the mixing of white and colored blood. The members of these societies are oath-bound to marry none but white women. This shows the pride of the Negro, who is unwilling to submit to racial bounds and the edicts of Holy Writ. He attempts to take matters in his own hands, but he will only bring calamity upon himself and his race for his presumption. God's laws governing the races are immutable, and woe unto the man who would try to change them.

The Negro's greatest asset is his simplicity of faith in the New Testament Gospel. When he tries to stretch himself beyond his measure he invariably gets into trouble. The Negro "spirituals" and the sermons of leading colored evangelists are everywhere popular and have done much good. In the days of slavery, many masters on their death-beds preferred to have the prayers and comfort of some pious slave rather than the services of the parish minister. Let the colored people keep in the place where God appointed them and save themselves from racial suicide and the judgments that would otherwise fall upon them and their posterity.

The KKK is misrepresented

The attitude of the Ku Klux Klan toward the colored people has been grossly and purposely misrepresented by Jews and Roman Catholics, who have used the daily press for their own selfish and political interests. The Negroes have been made to believe that the Klan is their avowed enemy, when nothing could be farther from the truth. All kinds of falsehoods have been propagated about Klan animosity toward them for which there has not been the slightest foundation. Many white people have not understood the source of such fabrications; but one acquainted with the iniquitous system of the Roman-Hebrew alliance needs no enlightenment. This un-American coalition of garbage-can politicians wants the colored man's vote, and it matters little to them how it is gotten.

The Book of Genesis . . . teaches the supremacy of the white race.

The Klan is a white, Protestant, Gentile organization whose principles stand as much for the liberty and protection of the colored people as for the white race. It may take years to disillusion them and the general public, where there has been so much misrepresentation, but time will wear down any wall of opposition and bring about the vindication of those who stand for truth and righteousness.

A lie is said to be short-lived, but too often it happens that its destructive work has been accomplished before it can be checked. The colored people have been made to believe that the Klan regalia was designed for the special purpose of intimidating and terrorizing them. Remarks of porters on railroad trains have convinced me of this. On a certain occasion a colored porter, from a Romanized community of Chicago, saw a picture of Klansmen in their robes and remarked, "If I was to see one of them comin' toward me at night I'd kill myse'f runnin'.'" Another was heard to say, "If ever I gits a letter from the Ku Kluxes I's gonna finish readin' dat letter on de train." And so the contagion has spread until the colored population is thoroughly imbued with the idea that the Klan is secretly watching their activities and planning to do them harm.

The Klan is opposed to violence

The Klan is opposed to mob violence and lynchings, and has succeeded in abolishing them in places where they were of frequent occurrence; and yet the patriots are charged with floggings and other cruelties where crimes have been committed by men in disguise. Before the Klan was ever heard of, criminals in disguise were active, both in the North and the South. There was scarcely a daily paper that did not give reports of these night-raiders. There was no one on whom to lay the blame until the Klan arose to safeguard our liberties.

The author could relate a number of instances in connection with her Church where Roman Catholics and Jews resorted to mob violence to keep Christian workers from exercising their constitutional rights in the worship of God. The latter were pelted with eggs and stones and driven from their places of worship by these men in disguise, aided by Roman Catholic police. One such occasion was at Plainfield, New Jersey, in 1915, where the offenders brandished revolvers in the faces of Protestant ministers and others, boarded trolley cars and trains and followed them for miles out of the city, after the police, standing in the shadows, had superintended the cutting down of the tent. Now from the same political sources comes the wholesale denunciation of the Knights of the Ku Klux Klan, laying to their charge acts of violence to prejudice the public mind. Governor Alfred E. Smith, the outstanding candidate for the presidential nomination by the Democratic Party, made known his opinion of the Klan in a letter dated December 29, 1927, to the Klan representative of Queen's County, Long Island. Governor Smith is quoted in the New York *World* of December 30 as saying: "I regard the purposes of your organization with abhorrence and I consider them subversive of the fundamentals of American democracy." Read the principles of the Klan . . . and consider whether you want a man elected president who abhors them.

12

White People Are the Creators of All Worthwhile Culture and Civilization

Matthew Hale

Matthew Hale is the Pontifex Maximus (supreme leader) of the World Church of the Creator.

The religion of "Creativity" is dedicated to the survival, expansion, and advancement of the white race. Non-Jewish white people have created all that is worthwhile in the world, and it is morally right that they have dominion over the earth. It is the philosophy of the World Church of the Creator to hate one's enemies—Jews and the "mud races"—and love one's own kind, the white race. Acting according to this creed is to the benefit and survival of all white people.

*W*ho is the "Creator"?
    The White Race. White people are the creators of all worthwhile culture and civilization. Also, believers in our racial religion are called Creators.
    If you were to sum up the objective of your religion, Creativity, in one sentence what would that be?
    That objective would be: The Survival, Expansion and Advancement of the White Race.
    Why is that so important?
    It is a matter of priorities. Our religion is based on the ultimate of all truths: The Eternal Laws of Nature. Nature tells each species to expand and upgrade itself to the utmost of its abilities. Since the White Race is Nature's finest achievement and since we encompass the White Race, there can hardly be any other goal that even compares in importance.
    As a rule, racists and anti-Semites reject those labels. You embrace them. Why?
    Because the first prerequisite to our attaining victory is to be completely honest about what we are and what we are not. We are racists be-

cause we believe in Race. We are anti-Semites because we oppose the Jews.

Isn't your religion based on hate?

No, on the contrary, it is based on love—love for the White Race. Besides being based on the Eternal Laws of Nature, Creativity furthermore is based on the lessons of history, on logic and common sense.

The World Church of the Creator is often described with words like "hate-monger," "hate organization," "hate speech." Is this fair?

No, it isn't fair since every organization—whatever it may be—hates something or someone. Since other organizations aren't labeled "hate" groups, etc., why should we be singled out like this? We don't exist out of hatred for the other races but out of love for our own Race.

But isn't it part and parcel of your religion to hate the Jews, blacks and other colored people?

True, but if you love and want to defend those whom you love, your own family, your own White Race; then hate for your enemies comes natural and is inevitable. Love and hate are two sides of the same coin. Only a hypocrite and a liar will go into battle against his enemies proclaiming love.

We don't exist out of hatred for the other races but out of love for our own Race.

But weren't all the atrocities committed by Christians throughout history done by people who were not following Christianity's teaching of love?

Since these killings, tortures, and persecutions were carried on by the highest leaders and authorities of the various Churches themselves, such as the Popes, by Zwingli, Luther, Calvin, etc., we must presume that the teachings of Christianity, which at best are ambiguous, contradictory and hypocritical, must be held responsible for producing these kinds of people and this kind of insanity. But if we turn to the New Testament, we find Christ himself dispensing such hateful advice as, for example, in Luke 14:26: "If any man come to me, and hate not his father, and mother and wife, and children, and brethren and sisters, yea and his own life also, he cannot be my disciple." What idiotic and destructive advice!

Love your race, hate your enemies

What then is Creativity's final position on love and hate?

We follow the eternal wisdom of Nature's laws, which are completely opposite to the suicidal teachings of Christianity. Whereas Christianity says to "love your enemies" and to hate your own kind (see, e.g., Luke 14:26), we say just the opposite. We say that in order to survive, we must overcome and destroy those that are a threat to our existence; namely, our deadly enemies. At the same time, we advocate love and protection for those that are near and dear to us: our family and our own race, which is an extension of the family.

How does this differ from Christianity?

Christianity teaches love your enemies and hate your own kind, while we teach exactly the opposite, namely hate and destroy your enemies and love your own kind. Whereas Christianity's teachings are suicidal, our creed brings out the best creative and constructive forces inherent to the White Race. Whereas Christians are destroyers, we are builders.

What do you mean about Christianity being a destroyer?

Christianity teaches such destructive advice as "love your enemies," "sell all thou hast and give it to the poor," "resist not evil," "judge not," "turn the other cheek." Anybody that followed such suicidal advice would soon destroy themselves, their family, their race and their country.

The aim of our religion . . . is promoting the best interests of our race, the White Race, which we believe is the highest pinnacle of Nature's creation.

If Christianity is as destructive as you say it is, how do you explain the fact that it has survived for nearly 2,000 years?

Smallpox has survived for longer than that, but the damage it has perpetrated on its victims has been devastating. Similarly, the creed and the church have survived for nearly 2,000 years, but the horrible damage it has wrought on the White Race is something else again. The Jews primary objective in concocting Christianity was to destroy their mortal enemies, the Roman Empire. In this they were successful beyond their wildest dreams. Two thousand years ago, before the advent of Christianity, the Roman Empire had reached an astoundingly high level of civilization, art, literature, law-giving, road building, language, and in dozens of other fields that are the hallmarks of progress in the White Man's civilization. Beginning with the reign of Augustus Caesar, Rome enjoyed two centuries of peace and prosperity (known as Pax Romana), the longest such span in history. As Christianity spread, and more and more poisoned the Roman mind, the good Roman citizens lost touch with reality and their minds meandered off into the "never-never land" of the spooks in the sky, fueled by fear of that humble torture chamber, HELL. The result was the collapse of the Roman Empire, and the White Race retrogressed into chaos, barbarism, and a thousand years of the Dark Ages. Poverty, ignorance and superstition were rampant. Like a monster, the Christian church fed upon and capitalized on these miseries. But the church itself grew fat and powerful. . . .

Promoting the best interests of the white race

What do you believe in?

Creativity is the Eternal Laws of Nature applied to all aspects of life, including and especially our Race. In order to get the full scope and breadth of our beliefs, you must read and study *Nature's Eternal Religion* and the *White Man's Bible*.

What, in substance, is that belief?

The aim of our religion, briefly, is promoting the best interests of our race, the White Race, which we believe is the highest pinnacle of Nature's creation.

Do you have a "Golden Rule" in your religion?

Yes, we do have a Golden Rule in our religion, and it does not coincide at all with the Golden Rule generally accepted in the Jewish-Christian philosophy. Our Golden Rule briefly can be summarized as follows: That which is good for the White Race is the highest virtue; that which is bad for the White Race is the ultimate sin.

Don't you believe in the commonly accepted Golden Rule of "Do unto others as you would have them do unto you"?

No, we do not, and the reason we don't is that when you analyze it more closely, just like many of the other shibboleths of the Jewish-Christian Bible, the so-called Golden Rule does not make good sense. To quote some examples: We would not treat our enemies the same way as we would treat our friends. Our relationship to our employees would not be the same as to our boss. Our relationship to our children would not be the same as that to our parents. Our relationship to members of the White Race would not be the same as to members of the black race, for instance and we would not expect the same kind of response. The number of examples that could be quoted are endless, and on closer analysis, it is a completely unworkable principle. . . .

Taking care of our own kind

Why do you limit your interest in the benefiting of the White Race only? Aren't you interested in all of humanity?

Nature tells us to take care of our own kind and only our own kind. We do not regard any of the mud races to be our own kind. They may be sub-species of some common ancestor, or they may not. In any case, we regard the White Race as having risen to the very top of the human scale, with varying graduations of subhuman species below us. The niggers, undoubtedly, are at the very bottom of the ladder, not far above monkeys and chimpanzees.

But couldn't your program be more charitable and help the other races advance, while at the same time promoting the White Race?

The answer to this rather tricky question is a most emphatic "NO!" We have no intention of helping the mud races prosper, multiply, and crowd us off the limited space of this planet.

Had America not pursued this program of pushing onward and crowding the Indian, we would never have built this great stronghold of the White Race which we now call America.

Why not?

In answering this question, we again go back to the basic Laws of Nature, which show that each species or sub-species has its natural enemies, and it is a cold hard fact of life that the most deadly enemies of the White Race are first of all the Jews, and secondarily, all the other mud races who are competing for food and living space on this limited planet. We have but two hard choices: (a) of either race-mixing and amalgamating with the mud peoples of the world, and thereby dragging down and destroying the White Race, or taking the course that the World Church of the Creator has chosen, namely, (b) to keep our own race pure and expand until we finally inhabit all the good lands of this planet Earth.

When the White Man is asked to show a loyalty to his own race, he is immediately denounced . . . as being a racist.

Wouldn't this entail a confrontation, in fact, a blood bath, in which the White Race might be wiped out?

Not necessarily. It is the program of the World Church of the Creator to keep expanding the White Race and crowding the mud races without necessarily engaging in any open warfare or without necessarily killing anybody. In doing so, we are only following the same principle as the colonization and westward expansion of America. During this great and productive epoch of the White Race, we kept expanding westward and onward by settling the lands that were occupied by an inferior human sub-species, namely, the Indians. It is true that there were some minor clashes, but there was not any open war of extermination. Had America not pursued this program of pushing onward and crowding the Indian, we would never have built this great stronghold of the White Race which we now call America. This is the real American way and we of the World Church of the Creator are expanding the American way on a worldwide basis.

Unite the white race

But isn't this cruel and inhuman?

No, it is not. It is just a matter of deciding whether you would rather have your own future progeny of beautiful, intelligent White people survive and inhabit this earth, or whether you would rather see them submerged in a flood tide of mud races. In the latter case, all beauty, culture and civilization would vanish. The more we help the mud races to expand and multiply, the more we are robbing our own future generations of food, space and existence on this planet Earth. Furthermore, the mud races are doing to us that very thing in the present stage of history. They have viciously driven out and killed the White population in many countries in Africa, and I might add with the connivance and help of Jews and White traitors. Our Jewish-controlled Government right here in America is promoting the expansion and proliferation of the niggers in the United States, and shrinking the White population so that in a few generations practically all of the United States will be either completely black or mongrelized. It is strange indeed that the bleeding hearts who are so concerned about the survival of the mud races seem to be completely unconcerned about the mongrelization and destruction of the White Race, a process that is now going on before our very eyes.

But in your book Nature's Eternal Religion, *aren't you actually advocating the extermination of the Jews?*

Nowhere in our book do we ever suggest killing anybody. Our program simply is to unite the White Race for its own survival and protection, expansion and advancement. It is because the White Race has flagrantly violated Nature's Laws of looking after its own, and stupidly and foolishly instead has subsidized the expansion and proliferation of our enemies, the multitudes of mud races, that we are now on a collision course with disaster. We Creators strongly advocate that we stop this foolishness of subsidizing our enemies, and let them shift for themselves, and we take care of our own.

But wouldn't this mean the decline and perhaps the extermination of the colored races?

Perhaps it would, but that is not our responsibility, nor is it our doing. Nature has decreed that every species on the face of this earth be engaged in a struggle for survival on its own merits in competition with every other species. In no case, in no species in Nature, does the stronger and superior species voluntarily hold itself back and help subsidize a weaker and inferior species so that inferior species might crowd it from the face of the earth. No other species, that is, except the White Race, is foolishly engaging in that kind of foolish philosophy. We Creators say that this is suicidal and that we must drastically change our course. Every individual, sooner or later, dies anyway, but it is a matter of the survival of our own species, our own kind, that we are interested in. Since there is not enough land, food, and substance to support an ever exploding horde of mud races, the vital question as we stated before is: do we want our own kind to survive, or do we want the suicide of our own future generations in a world flooded by the sub-human mud races? . . .

Do you hate police and military personnel?

No. The United States Iron Heel's military and police forces are evil institutions, but we have nothing against many individual cops and soldiers, who are often the best of our Race. Indeed, many cops and soldiers are sympathetic to the pro-White cause.

Why do you use the term "niggers" in your books instead of showing some respect for the blacks and calling them "Negroes"?

This is a deliberate choice of words. As we state on page 42 in *Nature's Eternal Religion,* we must stop giving them credit and respect which they did not earn, do not deserve, and never did. Again, it is very strange that the same people who are so affronted by the niggers not getting their "proper respect" are totally unconcerned about the vicious, unwarranted attacks by the niggers and other mud races upon the White Race and will not lift a finger in the defense of their own kind. They seem to deem it quite proper that the niggers should be loyal to their race, the Jews should be loyal to their race, but when the White Man is asked to show a loyalty to his own race, he is immediately denounced, even by members of his own race, as being a racist, a bigot, a Nazi, and many other derogatory smear words that the Jews have concocted.

Jews as no. 1 enemy

Why do you single out the Jews, who after all comprise less than one percent of the population of the world as your No. 1 enemy?

There are many good and valid reasons why the Jew deserves this special distinction. (a) The Jewish race, united through their Mosaic religion for thousands of years, has been for many centuries, and is today, the most powerful race on the face of the earth. (b) They not only control the news media, television networks, newspapers, and the money of the world, as of the United States, but through such power they also control the governments of the world. (c) They do, in fact, control most of the nerve centers of power in the United States and throughout the world. (d) It has been their age-old goal, not only for centuries, but for millennia, to pull down, mongrelize and destroy the White Race. (e) They have been very successful in doing this. We therefore conclude that they are a most dangerous threat to the further survival of the White Race.

If the Jews could organize the Christian church for the destruction of the White Race, surely the White Race can organize itself for its own survival.

Since you claim that your objectives do not include killing the Jews, just what do you propose?

It is our purpose to drive the Jews from power and eventually drive them from our shores back to Israel or whatever part of the world they choose to live in as a country of their own (perhaps also the island of Madagascar) without robbing other people of their established country.

How do you propose to do this?

By uniting and organizing the White race, and through the creed and program of the World Church of the Creator. By preaching and promoting racial loyalty among our own White Racial Comrades and making them conscious of their proud and wonderful heritage, we believe that we can mobilize the full power of the White Race and AGAIN REGAIN CONTROL OF OUR GOVERNMENT AND OUR OWN DESTINY. Once we have done that much, we believe that the fight against the Jews, the niggers and the mud races of the world is as good as won. Just distributing ten million copies of *Nature's Eternal Religion* and the *White Man's Bible* would put us well on the road to victory.

Didn't Hitler try to do the same thing and fail?

There are 500 million White people on the face of this planet. Organized and united they constitute an awesome power that would overwhelm the other peoples of the world, namely the mud races, in any kind of contest, or in any show of force. Whereas Hitler's program was similar to what we are proposing, we have learned from his failures and have made some significant changes. Whereas Hitler promoted and advocated pan-Germanism, namely, the German people as the core of his political movement, we, on the other hand, denounce Nationalism as an artificial barrier and a divisive force preventing the unification of the White Race. We promote and advocate the inclusion of all the good members of the White Race throughout the world, and propose to unite them in one solid battering ram under the banners of our religion. There are some other significant differences between our program and that of Adolf Hitler.

Why do you believe that a religious organization is a better means of accomplishing such objectives than a political party?

There are several reasons why we are convinced that we must have a religious base rather than a political party to do the job. (a) Religion embraces just about every aspect of a people's life—economies, morals, customs, law, government, education, eugenics, and above all, in our religion, the survival, expansion and advancement of our own race. (b) A political party, on the other hand, has a much narrower base. (c) Politics has a weaker appeal to an individual's loyalty. (d) Religion, on the other hand, has a much deeper and profound influence on the entire course of his life. (e) Furthermore, history shows that religions can and do last for thousands of years, whereas practically any other human organization, whether it be government, nations, financial corporations, political parties, or whatever, are relatively short-lived, some of them existing for a few years or even less, and then fading from the scene. Of the thousands of political parties that have come and gone, few have lasted longer than perhaps fifty years and very few longer than a hundred years. In contrast to this, the Jews' Mosaic religion has lasted for several thousand years and been the keystone of the survival of the Jewish race, not to mention the horribly destructive ramifications in the lives and destruction of other nations. . . .

Reeducating the white man

What do you consider the main difficulty in winning your struggle?

The main problem we have is not overcoming the niggers and the Jews, and the mud races in general, but reeducating the perverted and twisted thinking that has poisoned the minds of the White Race over the many centuries. Despite the fact that the White Race is the most intelligent creature in the fields of logic, mathematics, science, inventions, medicine, and hundreds of other creative and productive areas, yet when it comes to the questions of race and religion, the White Race seems to be strangely stupefied as if under the influence of a mind-warping drug. And, in a way, the White Man's mind is warped as if poisoned with drugs. And this poison is the propaganda that the Jew has foisted on the White Race for all these centuries. The most potent of all these propaganda poisons that had infiltrated the White Man's thinking is the Christian religion. So, our main problem is replacing that religion with a sound racial religion for our own survival, expansion and advancement. As soon as we are able to straighten out the White Man's thinking, we can regard our problems and our struggle as good as won. Placing ten million copies of *Nature's Eternal Religion* and the *White Man's Bible* in the hands of our White Racial Comrades would be a major step in that direction. What a bargain that would be for the White Race!

How do you propose to "straighten out the White Man's thinking," as you put it?

This is the most difficult part of the task, but not at all impossible. After all, going back to Adolf Hitler, we find that he was highly successful in changing the thinking of the German people from one of communism, despair, and self-destruction, to one of vibrant creativity, constructive productivity, and re-establishing a highly constructive faith in their own people. We believe we can do the same thing for the White peoples of the United States, by widespread promotion and distribution of our books *Nature's Eternal Religion* and the *White Man's Bible,* and following that up with a strongly organized World Church of the Creator. If the Jews could organize the Christian church for the destruction of the White Race, surely the White Race can organize itself for its own survival. We can do it and we will do it!

Does Creativity believe in God?

When you ask that question, it is as vague as asking: Do you believe in "Quantity X"? There are a million different versions of "God." There is the Jewish version—a vengeful God interested only in the welfare of the Jews and repeatedly killing and destroying the Jews' enemies. There is the God of the Mohammedans, Allah; there is the "loving" God of the Christians. Women's Lib says God is a female, the niggers say he is black. Then there is the hocus-pocus about the Holy Trinity—that of the father, son and holy ghost all rolled into one. Whereas most of these versions were concocted by man to take on the image of human form, other versions like the Church of Religious Science say God is an all pervading spirit, like the ether, not in the image of man at all. These are just a few versions out of millions. Actually even members of the same religious denomination differ widely and let their imaginations run rampant. But there is not a shred of evidence to back up any of this nonsense. The sum total of all these wild proclamations is that nobody has any facts to substantiate their claims, and the sum total knowledge about any so-called God is zero. We Creators, therefore, reject all this nonsense about angels and devils and gods and all the rest of this silly spook craft. We go back to reality, and back to the Eternal Laws of Nature, about which the White Man does have an impressive fund of knowledge. . . .

Since Creativity does not believe in a Supreme Being, nor in a life in the hereafter, how can you claim to be a religion at all?

We have every legitimate right to that claim. (a) The constitution in effect prohibits any authority, religious, secular or otherwise, from delineating what is, or what is not, a religion. In short, if you claim you are a religion it is as valid as any rival religion's claim. (b) One of Webster's many definitions of religion is: "A cause, principle, system of tenets held with ardor, devotion, conscientiousness, and faith: a value held to be of supreme importance." Our faith resides in the future of the White Race and our values are set forth in *Nature's Eternal Religion,* especially the SIXTEEN COMMANDMENTS. (c) There are several major religions that are known as Nontheistic. Among these are Confucianism, Taoism, Buddhism, some sects of Hinduism, and many others. Although they contain much mysticism and hocus-pocus we don't indulge in, the point is that they, too, do not believe in a God, but rather are socioethical systems proclaiming certain moral values. Yet they have been recognized as religions for centuries, and rightfully so. There are other valid reasons why we rightfully qualify as a religion, but the above should suffice.

Religion rooted in race

What kind of religion would you call yourself?

Our religion is rooted in race, and based upon the Eternal Laws of Nature. We are, therefore, a racial religion and a natural religion. . . .

Since you do not believe in God and you do not worship anything, what is the purpose of your religion?

We have set up the loftiest and most noble goal humanly possible, namely, the Survival, Expansion and Advancement of the White Race. If the White Race isn't worth the dedication of our most ardent labors, what is? Niggers and monkeys? Imaginary, non-existent spooks in the sky? In Creativity, we have given the White Race a great and noble purpose in life. We have given the White Race a program for its own salvation and advancement for the next million years. We have given our own race a creed around which all members of our race can rally, regardless of nationality. Finally, after thousands of years of floundering, divisiveness and self-destruction, the White Race now has a meaningful constructive religion upon which it can build a better world for itself and its future progeny forever and a day. . . .

Don't you have faith in anything?

Yes, we most certainly do. . . . We have faith in the future of the White Race and its ultimate triumph. We consider that as the highest and most significant goal. The fact is we believe in anything that has valid and meaningful evidence to substantiate it. . . . We do not believe in a world of spirits and spooks and we most certainly do not believe in the Jewish Bible which was written by a gang of lying, Jewish scriptwriters. We believe "A SKEPTICAL AND INQUIRING MIND IS NO VICE. BEING GULLIBLE AND SUPERSTITIOUS IS NO VIRTUE.". . .

Since you say that the Jews occupy all the nerve centers of power, just how do you propose to drive them from power and have the White Man regain control of his destiny?

We mean to do this by building and expanding the World Church of the Creator until it penetrates the thinking and the heart and soul of all the good members of the White Race. As we have stated before, our biggest problem really is straightening out the thinking of White People. We believe that it can be done and it must be done, in fact, by building a religious movement dedicated to the survival, expansion and advancement of the White Race. We believe it is the only way that this tremendous task can be accomplished. It can be done, and it will be done.

Among our enemies, we have the Jews and the mud races.

Doesn't Creativity believe in helping others?

Yes, we do, but we are highly selective as to whom we render aid, love and affection. We most definitely do not believe in loving enemies, nor helping them. Among our enemies, we have the Jews and the mud races. We, therefore, believe in selectively helping our own kind, namely, our own White Racial Comrades. The White Man is the measure of all things, and we believe in looking at everything through the White Man's eyes, from the White Man's point of view.

The Bible is a hoax

Hasn't the Bible been pretty well proven by recent scientific discoveries and isn't the gap between Christianity and science rapidly deteriorating?

Most definitely not. The answer to both questions is a loud emphatic, NO! The gap between Christianity and science is as wide as the Grand

Canyon. It is widening as science progresses in giant strides. The gap is irreconcilable and unbridgeable. A study of astronomy and the discovery of billions of other galaxies makes the idea of spooks in the sky a laughable absurdity. A study of geology makes the idea of a universal flood in the year 2348 B.C. a non-existent hoax. A study of Egyptian history also completely repudiates the story of the great flood. A study of authentic history further repudiates the so-called "history" the Jews have concocted for themselves in the Old Testament. Suffice it to say that the conflict is endless and an excellent set of books has been written on this subject. It comes in two volumes and is entitled *A History of the Warfare of Science with the Theology of Christendom* written by A.D. White. Unfortunately, it is now out of print and extremely hard to come by. . . .

The White Race is now a very much endangered species.

The White Race seems to have done quite well in maintaining itself. Why are you so concerned about its survival?

The White Race used to do quite well for itself in the 15th, 16th, 17th, 18th and 19th centuries, but no more. In fact, as late as 1920, the White Race was outnumbered by the mud races of the world only in a proportion of 2 to 1. Today, scarcely two generations later, it is outnumbered by the rapidly exploding mud races of the world, by a ratio of 12 to 1. The United Nations, which is a Jew-controlled organization, gleefully reports that in another generation the White Race will be outnumbered on the face of this earth by a ratio of 49 to 1. A person has to only have an elementary grasp of mathematics to see that the White Race is now a very much endangered species, and will soon be either crowded into extinction or mongrelized into oblivion. Either way, the White Race will be gone, and with it also will vanish all the good things that it has produced, such as civilization, culture, art and all the other valuable attributes that we consider as contributing to the good life. The tragic and ironic thing about all this is that it's the White Man's ability to produce ample food, the White Man's technology, the White Man's medicine, and all the other valuable contributions created by his own ability, foolishly transferred to the parasitic mud races that has caused the present dilemma arid catastrophe. It is these valuable contributions of the White Race transferred to the mud races that has caused the latter's explosive increase. It is the unalterable goal of the World Church of the Creator to bring the White Man back to sanity and to again conserve his creativity and productivity for the benefit of his own race and his race alone. . . .

Jewish lies

Does Creativity agree with Adolf Hitler in all respects?

Not in all respects. There are four or five major issues in which we depart from National Socialism. The main difference is we believe Nationalism, per se, was and is a divisive issue among the White Race. We instead espouse RACIAL SOCIALISM to embrace all the good White people on the face of the globe, rather than Pan-Germanism.

But didn't Hitler kill six million Jews?

No, he did not. This, along with Christianity, ranks as one of the biggest lies and biggest hoaxes in history. Privately, among themselves, the Jews published the growth of their total world population between 1938 and 1948, as increasing from approximately 16,600,000 to 17,650,000, an increase of over a million. This would be an outrageous impossibility, if it had been decimated by 6,000,000 during this same period.

If it isn't true, why would the Jews want to tell such a monstrous lie?

It has reaped tremendous dividends for them. Having worldwide monopoly of the propaganda machinery, they were able to put that lie across with little or no opposition.

What were the "tremendous dividends" for the Jews you speak of?

(a) It enabled the Jews who were the real instigators of World War II and the real culprits, to appear to be the victims, and arouse worldwide sympathy from the gullible and unsuspecting Gentiles, or Goyim, as they call them. (b) Through this world sympathy, it enabled them to loot the Arabs of their lands in Palestine, and set up the bandit State of Israel. (c) It enabled them to loot the Germans with "restitutions" in amounts of as much as a billion dollars a year to the State of Israel. In short, this is plain blackmail and looting. (d) It enabled them to pursue a vicious program of destroying all opposition to Jewish aggression and take-over throughout the world. (e) It has provided them with a bonanza in tightening their stronghold on the peoples of the world in areas of finances, of propaganda, of governmental expansion and the spread of Jewish Communism.

So what do you propose as the answer to the Jewish problem?

The only total answer is for the White people of the world to unite and organize and regain control of their own destiny. This is the highest right in Nature. In order to do so they have to unite around something and that something must be a meaningful, significant and worthwhile creed that all the good White people of this earth can dedicate their lives to. This we have provided in the religious creed of Creativity as set forth in *Nature's Eternal Religion* and the *White Man's Bible*. In it lies the philosophy, the creed and the program for the salvation of the White Race for its own survival, expansion and advancement for all time. It is every White Man's highest moral duty to promote, advance and disseminate this lofty creed, not only for his own generation, but also to our future progeny for the next million years. Therefore let us dedicate ourselves to this noble task and go to work. . . .

What does "RAHOWA" mean?

It is our battle cry. Just as the Muslims have "jihad," we have "RA-HOWA." It stands for RAcial HOly WAr.

Organizations to Contact

The editors have compiled the following list of organizations concerned with the issues debated in this book. The descriptions are derived from materials provided by the organizations. All have publications or information available for interested readers. The list was compiled on the date of publication of the present volume; the information provided here may change. Be aware that many organizations take several weeks or longer to respond to inquiries, so allow as much time as possible.

African Americans for Humanism (AAH)
PO Box 664, Buffalo, NY 14226
(716) 636-7571 • fax: (716) 636-1733
website: www.secularhumanism.org

AAH is dedicated to developing humanism in the secular African American community and fighting racism through humanistic education. It publishes the quarterly newsletter *AAH Examiner*.

American Civil Liberties Union (ACLU)
125 Broad St., 18th Fl., New York, NY 10004-2400
(212) 549-2500 • publications: (800) 775-ACLU (2258)
e-mail: aclu@aclu.org • website: www.aclu.org

The ACLU is a national organization that works to defend Americans' civil rights guaranteed by the U.S. Constitution. The ACLU publishes and distributes policy statements, pamphlets, and the semiannual newsletter *Civil Liberties Alert*.

Amnesty International (AI)
322 Eighth Ave., New York, NY 10001
(212) 807-8400 • (800) AMNESTY (266-3789) • fax: (212) 627-1451
website: www.amnesty-usa.org

Founded in 1961, AI is a grassroots activist organization that aims to free all nonviolent people who have been imprisoned because of their beliefs, ethnic origin, sex, color, or language. *The Amnesty International Report* is published annually, and other reports are available online and by mail.

Anti-Defamation League (ADL)
823 United Nations Plaza, New York, NY 10017
(212) 490-2525
website: www.adl.org

ADL works to stop the defamation of Jews and to ensure fair treatment for all U.S. citizens. It publishes the periodic *ADL Law Report* and *Law Enforcement Bulletin* as well as other reports.

Aryan Nations
Church of Jesus Christ Christian
PO Box 362, Hayden Lake, ID 83835
e-mail: aryannhq@nidlink.com • website: www.nidlink.com

Aryan Nations promotes racial purity and believes that whites are persecuted by Jews and blacks. It publishes the *Aryan Nations Newsletter* and pamphlets such as *New World Order in North America, Aryan Warriors Stand,* and *Know Your Enemies.*

Cato Institute
1000 Massachusetts Ave. NW, Washington, DC 20001-5403
(202) 842-0200 • fax: (202) 842-3490
website: www.cato.org

The Cato Institute is a libertarian public policy research foundation dedicated to limiting the role of government and protecting individual liberties. It researches claims of discrimination and opposes affirmative action. The institute publishes the quarterly magazine *Regulation,* the bimonthly *Cato Policy Report,* and numerous books.

Center for the Study of Popular Culture (CSPC)
9911 W. Pico Blvd., Suite 1290, Los Angeles, CA 90035
(310) 843-3699 • fax: (310) 843-3692
website: www.cspc.org

CSPC is a conservative educational organization that addresses topics such as political correctness, cultural diversity, and discrimination. Its civil rights project promotes equal opportunity for all individuals and provides legal assistance to citizens challenging affirmative action. The center publishes four magazines: *Heterodoxy, Defender, Report Card,* and *COMINT.*

Citizens' Commission on Civil Rights (CCCR)
2000 M St. NW, Suite 400, Washington, DC 20036
(202) 659-5565 • fax: (202) 223-5302
e-mail: citizens@cccr.org • website: www.cccr.org

CCCR monitors the federal government's enforcement of antidiscrimination laws and promotes equal opportunity for all. It publishes reports on affirmative action and desegregation as well as the book *One Nation Indivisible: The Civil Rights Challenge for the 1990s.*

Commission for Racial Justice (CRJ)
700 Prospect Ave., Cleveland, OH 44115-1110
(216) 736-2100 • fax: (216) 736-2171

CRJ was formed in 1963 by the United Church of Christ in response to racial tensions gripping the nation at that time. Its goal is a peaceful, dignified society where all men and women are equal. CRJ develops many programs for racial and ethnic United Church of Christ churches that help them meet the needs of their individual communities. CRJ also publishes various documents and books, such as *Racism and the Pursuit of Racial Justice* and *A National Symposium on Race and Housing in the United States: Challenges for the 21st Century.*

Euro-American Alliance
PO Box 2-1776, Milwaukee, WI 53221
(414) 423-0565

This organization opposes racial mixing and advocates self-segregation for whites. It publishes a number of pamphlets, including *Who Hates Whom?* and *Who We Really Are.*

The Heritage Foundation
214 Massachusetts Ave. NE, Washington, DC 20002-4999
(202) 546-4400 • fax: (202) 546-0904

The foundation is a conservative public policy research institute dedicated to free-markct principlcs, individual liberty, and limited government. It opposes affirmative action and believes that the private sector, not government, should be allowed to ease social problems and to improve the status of women and minorities. The foundation publishes the quarterly journal *Policy Review* and the bimonthly newsletter *Heritage Today* as well as numerous books and papers.

Hispanic Policy Development Project (HPDP)
1001 Connecticut Ave. NW, Suite 901, Washington, DC 20036
(202) 822-8414 • fax: (202) 822-9120

HPDP is a nonprofit organization that encourages analysis of public policies affecting Hispanic youth in the United States, especially in education, employment, and family issues. It publishes a number of books and pamphlets, including *Together Is Better: Building Strong Partnerships Between Schools and Hispanic Parents.*

National Alliance
PO Box 90, Hillsboro, WV 24946
(304) 653-4600
website: www.natall.com

The alliance believes in white superiority and advocates the creation of a white nation free of non-Aryan influence. It publishes the newsletter *Free Speech* and the magazine *National Vanguard.*

National Association for the Advancement of Colored People (NAACP)
4805 Mt. Hope Dr., Baltimore, MD 21215-3297
(410) 358-8900 • fax: (410) 486-9257

The NAACP is the oldest and largest civil rights organization in the United States. Its principal objective is to ensure the political, educational, social, and economic equality of minorities. It publishes the magazine *Crisis* ten times a year as well as a variety of newsletters, books, and pamphlets.

National Association for the Advancement of White People (NAAWP)
PO Box 1727, Callahan, FL 32011
(904) 766-2253 • (813) 274-4988 • fax: (904) 924-0716
e-mail: naawp1@mediaone.net • website: www.naawp.org

NAAWP is a nonviolent, civil rights organization for white rights. It perceives Caucasians as being discriminated against in favor of special interest minority groups. The association, which seeks to preserve a white heritage, discourages interracial relationships. *NAAWP News* newsletter is published eight to ten times per year.

Poverty and Race Research Action Council (PRRAC)
1711 Connecticut Ave. NW, Suite 207, Washington, DC 20009
(202) 387-9887 • fax: (202) 387-0764
e-mail: prrac@aol.com

PRRAC is a national organization that promotes research and advocacy on be-half of poor minorities. It publishes the bimonthly newsletter *Poverty & Race.*

The Prejudice Institute
Stephens Hall Annex, TSU, Towson, MD 21204-7097
(410) 830-2435 • fax: (410) 830-2455

The Prejudice Institute is a national research center concerned with violence and intimidation motivated by prejudice. It conducts research, supplies in-formation on model programs and legislation, and provides education and training to combat prejudicial violence. The Prejudice Institute publishes re-search reports, bibliographies, and the quarterly newsletter *Forum.*

Stormfront
PO Box 6637, West Palm Beach, FL 33405
(561) 833-0030 • fax: (561) 820-0051
e-mail: comments@stormfront.org • website: www.stormfront.org

This organization promotes white superiority and serves as a resource for white political and social action groups. It publishes the weekly newsletter *Stormwatch*, and its website contains articles and position papers.

U.S. Commission on Civil Rights
624 Ninth St. NW, Suite 500, Washington, DC 20425
(202) 376-7533 • publications: (202) 376-8128

A fact-finding body, the commission reports directly to Congress and the president on the effectiveness of equal opportunity laws and programs. A cat-alog of its numerous publications can be obtained from its Publication Man-agement Division.

Bibliography

Books

Elliot Abrams — *Faith or Fear: How Jews Can Survive in a Christian America.* New York: Free Press, 1997.

Katherine Blee — *Inside Organized Racism: Women in the Hate Movement.* Berkeley: University of California Press, 2001.

Patrick Buchanan — *The Death of the West: How Dying Populations and Immigrant Invasions Imperil Our Country and Civilization.* New York: Dunne Books, 2001.

Betty A. Dobratz — *The White Separatist Movement in the United States: White Power, White Pride.* Baltimore: Johns Hopkins University Press, 2000.

David Duke — *My Awakening: A Path to Racial Awakening.* Mandeville, LA: Free Speech Press, 1998.

Laura K. Egendorf, ed. — *Anti-Semitism.* San Diego: Greenhaven Press, 1999.

George M. Frederickson — *Racism: A Short History.* Princeton: Princeton University Press, 2002.

Mark S. Hamm — *In Bad Company: America's Terrorist Underground.* Boston: Northeastern University Press, 2001.

S.T. Joshi, ed. — *Documents of American Prejudice: An Anthology of Writings on Race from Thomas Jefferson to David Duke.* New York: Basic Books, 1999.

Nick Knight — *Skinhead.* New York: Omnibus, 1997.

Albert S. Lindemann — *Esau's Tears: Modern Anti-Semitism and the Rise of the Jews.* New York: Cambridge University Press, 1997.

Andrew MacDonald (William Pierce) — *The Turner Diaries.* Fort Lee, NJ: Barricade Books, 1996.

Lou Michel — *American Terrorist: Timothy McVeigh and the Tragedy at Oklahoma City.* New York: Regan Books, 2002.

Chester L. Quarles — *The Ku Klux Klan and Related American Racialist and Anti-Semitic Organizations: A History and Analysis.* Jefferson, NC: McFarland, 1999.

Tamara L. Roleff — *Hate Groups.* San Diego: Greenhaven Press, 2001.

Ben Sonder — *The Militia Movement: Fighters of the Far Right.* Danbury, CT: Franklin Watts, 2000.

Carol M. Swain — *Challenges to an Integrated America: Emerging White Nationalism and Its Threat to Society.* New York: Cambridge University Press, 2002.

Strobe Talbott, ed.   *The Age of Terror: America and the World After September 11.* New York: Basic Books, 2002.

Jerome Walters   *One Aryan Nation Under God: Exposing the New Racial Extremists.* Cleveland: The Pilgrim Press, 2000.

Periodicals

Richard D. Barton   "A Free Nation Can Overcome Forces of Hate," *San Diego Union-Tribune,* August 15, 1999.

Omer Bartov   "Defining Enemies, Making Victims: Germans, Jews, and the Holocaust," *American Historical Review,* June 1998.

Robert O. Blanchard   "The 'Hate State' Myth," *Reason,* May 1999.

Jamie Byd   "Hate Kills," *Seventeen,* June 1999.

Lynette Clemetson   "The New Victims of Hate," *Newsweek,* November 6, 2000.

Ellis Cose   "The Good News About Black America," *Newsweek,* June 7, 1999.

David Cullen   "Bullies in the Pulpit," *In These Times,* November 29, 1998.

Susan Estrich   "The Threat Posed by Hate Groups," *Liberal Opinion Week,* August 23, 1999.

Michael Fletcher   "Interracial Marriages Eroding Barriers," *Washington Post,* December 28, 1998.

Gary Greenebaum   "Racists Can Justify Anything, Even Child Murder," *Liberal Opinion Week,* August 23, 1999.

David Lehrer   "Tolerance, Not Hate, Is on the Rise," *Los Angeles Times,* August 13, 1999.

Michael Lind   "The Beige and the Black," *New York Times Magazine,* August 16, 1998.

Sarah McCarthy   "Fertile Ground for Terrorists?" *Humanist,* January/February 1999.

Greg Steinmetz   "Hitler's Heirs: German Skinhead Tells Court, 'I Am a Racist,' as Neo-Nazis Spread," *Wall Street Journal,* August 3, 1998.

Jo Thomas   "New Face of Terror Crimes: 'Lone Wolf' Weaned on Hate," *New York Times,* August 16, 1999.

Washington Post   "The Aryan Nations Verdict," September 16, 2000.

Index